P9-CEP-149

JOSEPHINE COX

CHILD OF THE NORTH

MEMORIES OF A NORTHERN CHILDHOOD

JOSEPHINE COX

CHILD OF THE NORTH

PIERS DUDGEON WITH JOSEPHINE COX

HEADLINE

First published in 2001
by HEADLINE BOOK PUBLISHING

10 9 8 7 6 5 4 3 2 1

British Library Cataloguing in Publication Data
Dudgeon, Piers
Child of the North: a biography of Josephine Cox and her novels
1. Cox, Josephine 2. Women novelists, English - 20th century - Biography
3. Novelists, English - 20th century - Biography
I. Title
823.9'14
ISBN 0 7553 1004 7

Written, designed and produced by Piers Dudgeon
Printed by Tien Wah Press (PTE.) Limited, Singapore

HEADLINE BOOK PUBLISHING
A division of Hodder Headline
338 Euston Road
London NW1 3BH

www.headline.co.uk
www.hodderheadline.com

Contents

Introduction
by Josephine Cox 7

Regional Map (2001) 14

Prologue 15
Town Map (1882) 17

1 Early Days 20
Street Map (1931) 27
Street Map (1939) 55
Escape 77
Ritual 90

2 Stratagem & Strife 103
The Spirit of Industry 150

3 Broken Hearts 173

Books by Josephine Cox 190

Index 191

Acknowledgements 192

INTRODUCTION by JOSEPHINE COX

I thought I knew all there was to know about the land of my birth. I now realise that I was wrong.

This wonderful, in-depth book, meticulously researched and written by Piers Dudgeon, has opened my eyes to a world I never really knew, with the many places and events that were inevitably beyond my experience. My own private, precious little world was the back streets of Blackburn town, and the magical Corporation Park, where I played out many childish dramas in my mind and imagination.

Deprived and confined though my world was, it was never quiet or uneventful, and for all its inherent difficulties, I would not want to change it. I could never deny my upbringing, because it is who I am; my roots are firmly embedded in those difficult, frustrating, wonderful days, when food was short and 'nice' clothes were what someone else wore.

It has been said that your childhood moulds and makes you the person you are, and I believe this is true. It's why today, and for the rest of my life, I will never take things for granted. Each and every

'These narrow cobbled streets, flanked by narrow little houses, seemed a world away from their high-born neighbours... In times of good and bad, these close-knit communities looked out for each other. Every family knew every other family, and every mother looked out for every child.' Somewhere, Someday

'This street in Somewhere, Someday (Addison Street, left), *I used to play in that street when I was a child, and it is on a real steep brew, you know? The family of the children I played with used to live in the house at the very top. We were on a tour up north about four years ago and as we drove past the top of the street I saw this house all boarded up. And I thought, where have they gone? And if they've moved on, why is that house not being lived in? And it played on my mind because it was part of my life. So that is where the story came from.'*

value and principle I nurture, has sprung directly from my background. Added to that, it gave me the stories I write; stories of

'She had always seen Blackburn market as a magic carpet...when a body climbed aboard it would be transported to another world...a fairytale world where round every corner a new adventure awaited... Tossed into the hub of activity and camouflaged beneath the great umbrellas of red and white awnings which covered every stall down every avenue, touching each other until the sky itself was obliterated by this spreading, billowing roof, Queenie took delight in all about her...

Queenie in Her Father's Sins

It was then 'a fairytale world where round every corner a new adventure awaited...'

human beings, and emotions, and the knowledge that when life knocks you down, the only way back is to stand tall and straight and look it in the eye.

The whole of my childhood is like a moving picture in my mind. I loved every inch of the narrow cobbled streets. With their many pubs and churches, pawn shops and little houses, they throbbed with life. The square-headed, black-coated lamps quietly guarded the pavements by day and lit the way home for lovers and drunks of a night-time. The back-to-back houses with their tiny Coronation Street yards and cold, outside damp lavvies (situated in a discrete corner beside the midden hole) held many a naughty or dangerous secret behind the twitching net curtains. Secrets I carried into my adult life and which I now retell in my stories.

The people were warm and friendly, and every mother was mother to every child in the street; regardless of which house a child might live in. The men worked hard and the women bore the children, and life was hectic and noisy, and often violent.

Our own house bustled with children, but, thinking back, I was never really a child. That would have been far too easy.

My Blackburn was a wonderful place, with smoking chimneys that darkened the skies and mill whistles piercing the air, calling the folk to work. These 'folk' were 'real' flesh and blood people; a great number of the same kind of people remain to this

'All the ragged kids went to the Blackburn Ragged School. Although there was a lot of laughter and we made our own fun, the hardship was always there and we often went hungry. If there wasn't much money coming in at the end of the week, we'd go hungry. But I thought that was how life was.'

day; though many of the familiar landmarks I knew have long since gone. There was a loud, colourful market where the men shouted their wares, and the women from the seaside would sell their shrimps and other shellfish from the depths of a wicker basket.

The market was large and sprawling, with a splendid, sturdy clock that stood tall and proud in the centre, and could be seen from one corner of the marketplace to the other. On a weekend evening, its large smiling face looked down on the meeting of friends and sweethearts. No doubt it could have told many a tale which we will never know, because sadly, some years later, the planners in their infinite 'wisdom' saw fit to demolish this wonderful landmark.

There were other memorable 'landmarks' in my young life... The Ragged School, where Christian people offered practical help and comfort to the children from poorer backgrounds than their own. There was the Cicely Bridge Mill, where I would go to meet our Mam after school; and Nazareth House, where she would take us when things were not going so well financially...the nuns there were kind and generous, something I have never forgotten. There was the slaughter-house, near where, for some time, we lived...the awful smell permeated the air day and night; this is one particular memory I would prefer to erase, but which, like the other, is stored in my soul for all time.

One other unforgettable incident happened on a chilly morning in February 1952. I was playing in the street, when suddenly everybody rushed out of their houses, some in tears and others eager to spread the shocking news, that King George had died.

The street went into mourning, as did the whole country, but to me and every other child, it was something that affected only the adults; we looked and wondered, and cried when our parents cried; but being children, we did not seem directly touched by this sad, historic event. And yet it is a day I will never forget, because of the emotion that swept my little world and, for a time, carried me along.

Many years later, circumstances beyond my control carried me away from my beloved Blackburn, and in the doing, brought me together with Ken, my sweetheart and subsequently my husband and friend.

It is well known how my family means a great deal to me. In spite of my mam and dad going their different ways, I remain ever close to my sisters and the brothers it broke my heart to leave behind. I love them all now as I did then: without reservation.

I give my heartfelt thanks to Piers Dudgeon for his hard work and memorable account of the North of England in this book. I know he spent many hours driving about and walking the streets of Blackburn, researching wherever he could and chatting to anyone who had things to tell him. At the end of it, he has written a very special account of the way it was; and I, for one, am proud to be part of it all.

Josephine Cox, May, 2001

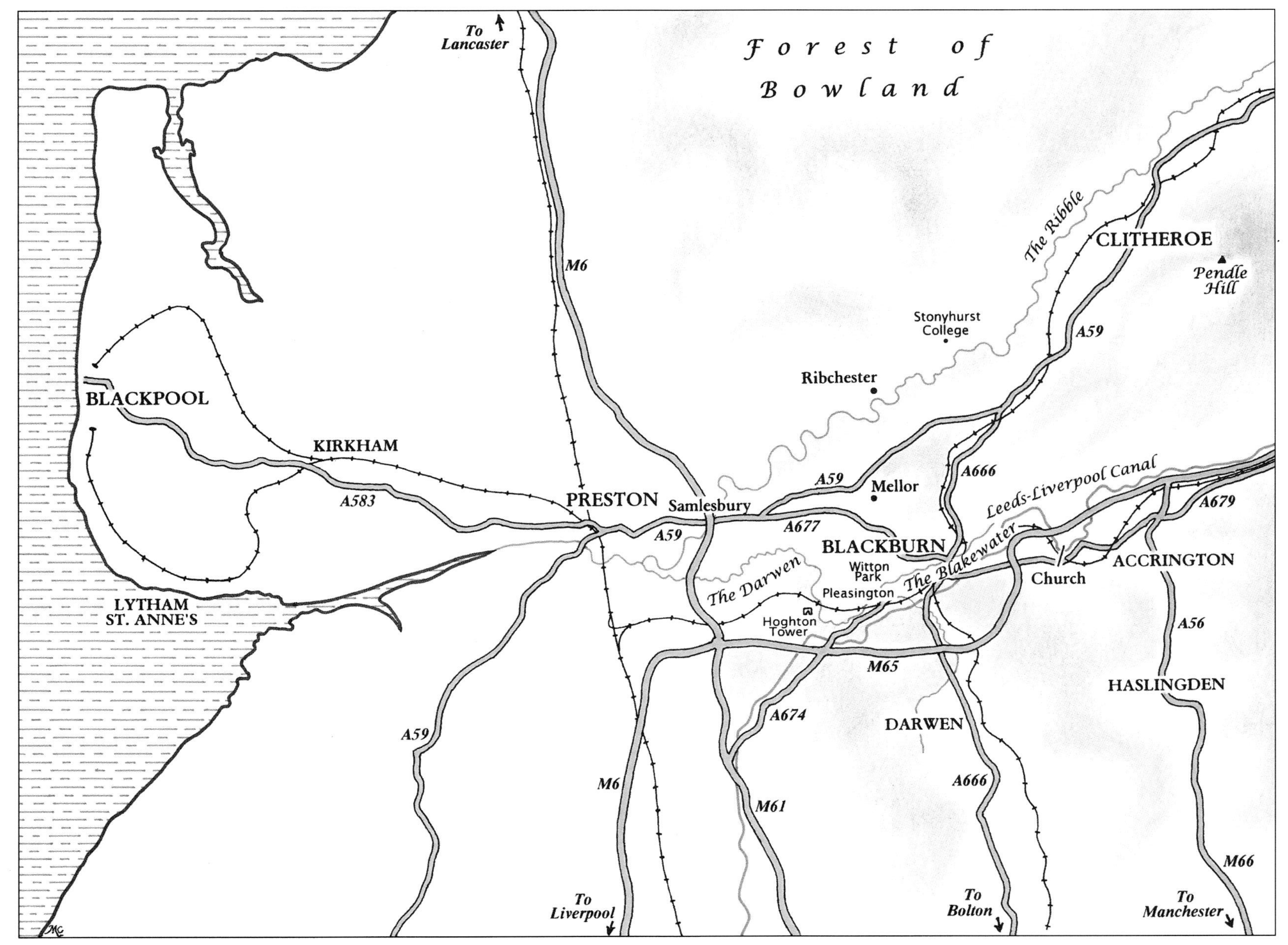
To Lancaster
Forest of Bowland
M6
CLITHEROE
The Ribble
Pendle Hill
Stonyhurst College
A59
Ribchester
BLACKPOOL
KIRKHAM
A583
PRESTON
Samlesbury
A59
Mellor
A666
Leeds-Liverpool Canal
A679
A677
BLACKBURN
Witton Park
Pleasington
The Blakewater
The Darwen
Church
ACCRINGTON
LYTHAM
ST. ANNE'S
Hoghton Tower
A56
M65
HASLINGDEN
A674
DARWEN
A59
M6
A666
M61
M66
To Liverpool
To Bolton
To Manchester

Prologue

On the face of it, there was little to entice the earliest treckers across the marshy landscape of West Lancashire into the scoop of land where Blackburn lies today beneath its very own cloud, dark, low and very wet. The town straddles the Blakewater, or Blackwater as it was once called, an idle, if occasionally irrepressible river, which readily concedes to the beauty of the nearby reaches of the West Pennine Moors.

The Romans were certainly blind to any 'special something' when checking out the valley for a garrison base. Ignoring the site, they drove on five miles to the north into the fells, and chose instead Ribchester (Bremetennacum) in the beautiful Ribble Valley. But their road builders did make a road between Ribchester and Manchester (Mamucium) to the south, breasting the Blakewater by means of a safe ford (later Sal-ford), from which Blackburn town would grow.

If Blackburn started out uninterestingly as the Roman equivalent of a motorway service station, the settlement which sprang up soon developed an impressive spirit of its own. In 596 AD the Saxons built a church there, dedicated to St Mary the Virgin. Rebuilt in the 14th century, and again in 1826, it became a cathedral in 1926. The Normans also had a presence, although, with outsider lack of vision, the de Lacys, who had been part of William the Conqueror's invasion force, preferred to base themselves at a castle in Clitheroe, again to the north.

From Salford, the town spread west through Church Street and King Street, north up North Gate and Shire Brow (now Shear Brow), and south down Darwen Street, as the 1822 map (page 17) shows. In medieval times, the market cross and punishment stocks were set where these roads intersected, the cross reduced to 'the Blackburn stump' by boisterous

The beautiful Ribble Valley just to the north of Blackburn, which lured the Romans into building a centre of operations at Ribchester, where, hard by the parish church (below), *there is a museum charting the Roman occupation.*

parliamentarians in the Civil War, when a local royalist, Sir Gilbert Hoghton of Hoghton Tower, was put to flight following skirmishes up and down Darwen Street and Church Street.

The town had by this time already set out on its 800-year industrial history, operating first in the 13th-century wool trade, until, in Elizabethan times, *fustian* came on the scene. Fustian was a cheaper, lighter cloth than wool, being a cotton weft and linen warp (the latter made with flax from Ireland). The soft water from the hills surrounding Blackburn, and its damp climate, turned out to be an excellent environment for spinning and weaving, and pretty soon the town's weavers had developed their own version of the cloth – blue and white 'Blackburn Checks' (later the colours of the local football team, Blackburn Rovers). Eventually this was superseded by an undyed, linen-and-cotton weave, known as 'Blackburn Greys', on which the extraordinary, 19th-century textile export boom would be based.

As early as the 16th century, Blackburn had been a flourishing market town of about 2,000 inhabitants. Five cattle and horse fairs were held annually, the oldest dating from 1583. By 1907, however,

Salford Bridge (right), *where Blackburn began, the 'safe ford' of Roman times. Eventually the town spread to cover the Blakewater almost completely. Townsman Graham Francis remembers how he and his mates used to light a fire in a dustbin lid and send it through a culverted stretch, watching for the first flicker of fire from the other end.*

The map (below) *shows Blackburn in 1822, when the street where Jo was born, west of where Princess Street meets King Street, was still green field.*

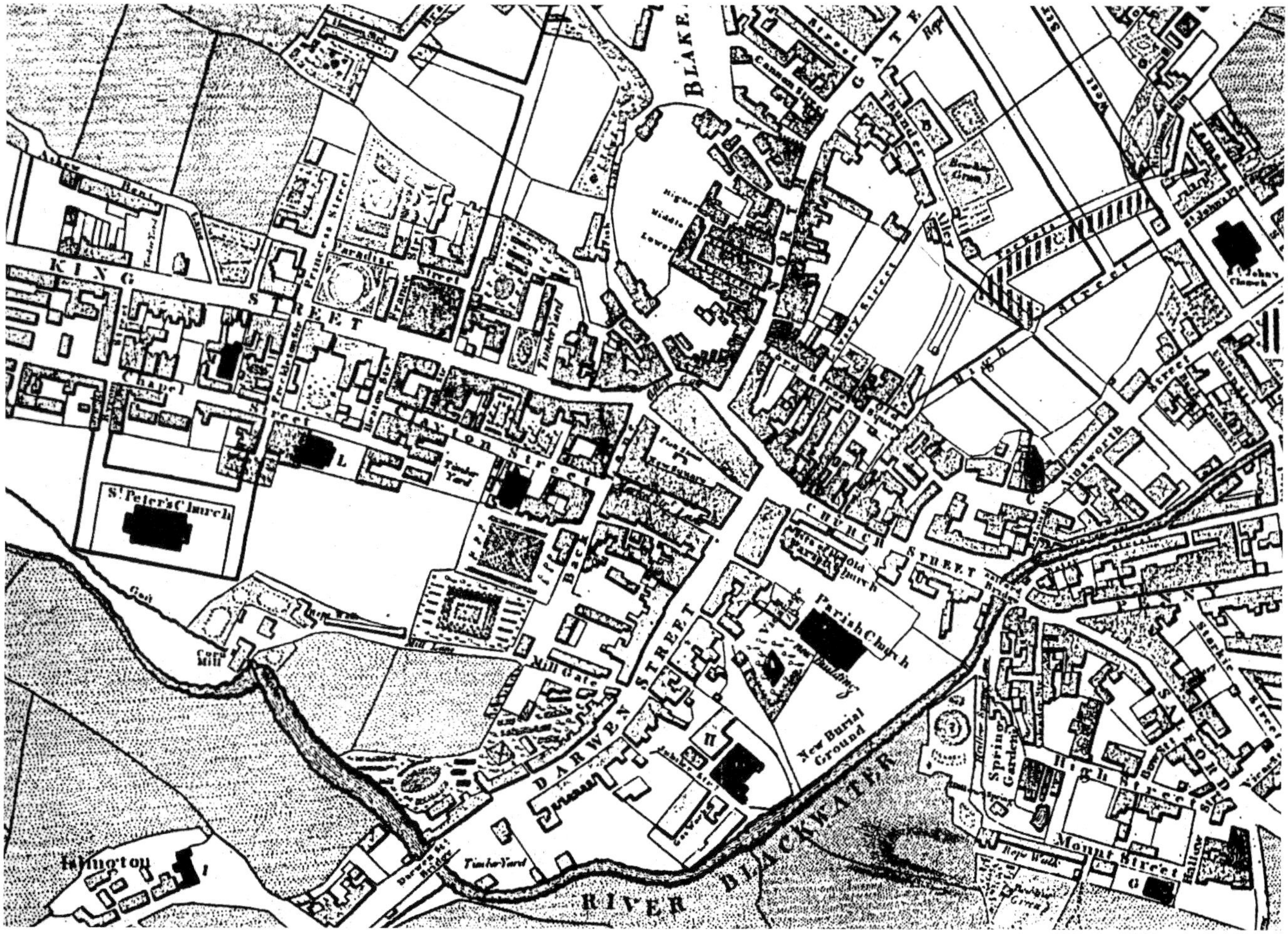

it was 'the cotton weaving capital of the world,' with a 6,500% population increase and an incredible 79,403 power looms in use.

In the intervening years, as we shall see, it sustained a quite extraordinary history of revolution, violence, prosperity, poverty, even starvation, before it began its painful and terminal wind-down, which saw in 1930 up to 50% of the workforce unemployed and, by 1957, a two-thirds reduction of its cotton mills, right down to one working mill – Witton Mill in Stancliffe Street – all that is left today.

The first mill-worker housing sprang up around Wensley Fold, Blackburn's first spinning mill, west of where Josephine Cox was born. Seven cottages appeared in 1809, numbers rapidly increasing so that by 1832 the mill master owned eighty-four houses around and about.

The burgeoning worker colonies comprised endless, closed-in rows of terraced housing, two rooms upstairs, two rooms down, no bath-

Above: *one of the earliest 19th-century mill colonies grew up around Nova Scotia Mill to the south west of the town, another was Brookhouse to the east, both beyond the confines of the 1822 map, page 17.*

Right: *These colonies were built to order, populated and then factory-farmed for their labour.*

The mill owned your house, the shops in the area and the pub at the end of the road. The master paid your wages and then mopped them up again in any way he could. Fortunes were made by the few on the backs of many.

room, no hot water except that which is boiled in the kettle, no front garden, a backyard scarcely big enough to turn round in and an outside lavatory backing onto a narrow passage.

Some of the earliest terraces were back-to-backs with no alleyway between, but it soon became apparent that these posed appalling sanitation and health risks.

Each house had a back yard scarcely big enough to turn round in, an outside lavatory backing onto a narrow passage and no hot water except that which is boiled in the kettle.'Mrs Aspen kept a wooden box by the back yard wall. Whenever she noticed Queenie hanging out the washing, she'd hoist her fat little form onto the box and stretch her short neck to peep over.' Her Father's Sins

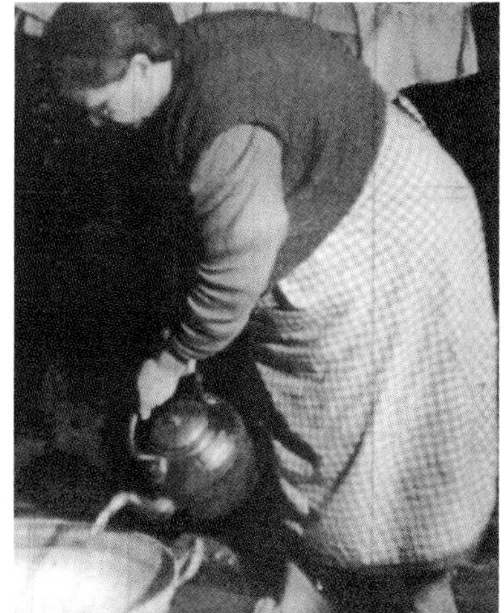

1 Child of the North: Early Days

'My earliest memories...sitting on the front doorstep, watching...'

'I was born in Derwent Street in Blackburn, Lancashire, during the Second World War, and my earliest memories are of sitting on the front doorstep, watching the world being created in that street.

'I would see kids playing, men fighting, sweethearts having a tiff and then making up, and I'd just sit and watch them, soaking it all in. If I close my eyes now I can still see it, just as if I were that five-year-old again. All the stories I have ever written have come from those people.'

The street was long, but straight like the lines of a railway track, lit by the tall blue-framed gas-lamps, which winked and sparkled at regular intervals on either side. From No. 2, which was right at the neck of the street, a body could look along the continuous row of tightly packed houses and experience the same sensation as if standing at the mouth of a long meandering tunnel.

The world that met Josephine Cox's curious stare from the doorstep of her house in the working-class Blackburn community of the 1940s and early '50s was still, as she noted in her first novel (*Her Father's Sins*, quoted above) – 'the old Lancashire, steeped in a tradition of cotton and ale –

Derwent Street was like any other street in the working-class Blackburn community of the 1940s and '50s. 'A narrow, cobbled street with tightly packed rows of thin grubby doors that opened straight out onto the pavement, it was noisy, dirty, swarming with people, but wonderfully welcoming. The women, laughing or talking, and nearly all pregnant, were busy white-stoning the steps, washing the windows, or watching young 'uns, who spent their days sitting on the kerbs with sugar butties; sailing matchstick boats down the gutters; and dropping loose stones into the stinking drains.

'"Hey up!" Smiling Tilly Shiner was the first to spot her. "It's young Laura!"'

Take This Woman

A Lancashire unwelcoming and unresponsive to the gentle nudging wind of change... Change would come, of that there could be no doubt. The old narrow houses with their steep unhygienic backyards, pot-sinks and outside lavvies, they wouldn't escape... But for now, Aunty Biddy's Blackburn remained relatively intact and contented and fiercely defended by every man, woman and child, who had never experienced any other way. They delighted in the open-topped rattling trams, the muffin-man's familiar shout, as he pushed his deep wicker basket along the uneven cobbles, and the screech of the cotton-mill siren, starting another day. As long as one and all were left alone to make their own way, they bothered nobody and asked no favours. The children spilled out to all the streets, played with their skipping-ropes, hula-hoops and spinning tops, their laughter no less spontaneous because of inherent poverty...

Her Father's Sins was about the way things were, the good times and the bad times; it is richly autobiographical. Queenie is the name of the little girl who experiences so many of the joys and traumas of Jo's early life on the streets of Blackburn. Although her home has been transferred from Derwent Street to Parkinson Street in the Mill Hill area of the town, they are, in many ways, interchangeable.

Lying in the half-dark, Queenie found it hard to settle. She sensed something was wrong. But what? After a while she dismissed the notion, and turned over to warm Auntie Biddy's side of the bed. But the uneasiness within her persisted. And slipping out from underneath the persuasive warmth of the eiderdown, she crossed to the window. For a change Parkinson Street was all quiet, save for the pitiful mewing of a frustrated tom cat, and the occasional dustbin-lid clattering to the flagstones beneath some scampering cat's feet.

Queenie looked along the higgledy-piggledy Victorian sky-line. The irregular pattern of chimneys reaching up like the fingers of a deformed hand traced a weird but comfortingly familiar silhouette against the moonlit sky. Lifting the window up against the sash, Queenie leaned out so she had an unobstructed view of the street below. Parkinson Street was home: No. 2, Parkinson Street, and Auntie Biddy, they were hers, her comforting world into which she could retreat when things became complicated and painful.

Class levels are defined by the number of gas lamps that 'line the pavements like smart grey soldiers in salute, proudly wearing the emblem of the Lancashire Rose on their shoulders...' Jessica's Girl

'I loved the street lamps and the cobbles,' Jo muses when we first meet. 'Many was the time I counted the cobbles in our street. When I had counted them from one end to the other, I counted the fanlights, the stained glass, on the way back. I had Queenie doing that.'

910 cobbles were counted 'up to Widow Hargreaves at No. 16'.

There were one hundred and four houses in Parkinson Street – Queenie had counted them all with loving precision. And there were one thousand and forty flagstones; Queenie had hopscotched every single one. She hadn't finished counting the road-cobbles yet, but up to Widow Hargreaves at No. 16, there were nine hundred and ten; that was counting across the road to the opposite houses. When she'd finished them, she would start on the stained glasses in the fanlight above the doors. Queenie meant to learn all there was to know about Parkinson Street because the more she knew, the more it was hers.

Stretching her neck, now, Queenie attempted to identify the dark figure approaching against the flickering gas-lamps. The tottering speck grew and grew, until it shaped itself into the towering frame of George Kenney. On recognising it, Queenie involuntarily backed away...

Parkinson Street, the imaginative theatre of Jo's real childhood joys and fears, exists today and has its own place in memory. 'We would go

The Mill Hill area may have changed, but it is easy enough even today to catch a glimpse of how it once was. To the right of the picture is the bridge where the urchin Molly escapes from a prison wagon in Alley Urchin.

'"Travel light, that's the best thing ter do, me darlin'," chuckled Sal, "then yer can tek ter yer heels if needs be, eh?" She tousled the girl's short, unkempt hair. "Mek towards the canal, up by Angela Street," she said, shuffling towards the door. "Happen the landlord at the Navigation might slip us a glass o' some'at strong . . ."'

Alley Urchin

up there as often as we could. We had relatives there, Auntie Margaret lived up there and we'd go and see her. My brother, Bernard, lived for many years in Stephen Street. And another brother, Richard, lived on Parkinson Street, so we were always up there. I love that area of old Mill Hill, and I have set a lot of my stories there. It has changed now obviously – you've got the Indian takeaway and all that, they weren't there; it was just little shops and little houses and cobbled streets, and I loved it.'

Mill Hill, to the south west of the town centre, developed in the latter part of the 19th century around Cardwell and Albert mills between the railway and the canal, together with another worker colony around Waterfall Mill in this same area, close to Parkinson Street. The area may have seen change, but it is easy enough even today to catch a glimpse of how it was. The Navigation itself hasn't changed at all, although, as I write, it is about to undergo a makeover. 'It's so old,' agrees Jo, 'and it's got the wooden benches around the wall and the real old characters, and my god you pick up some tales.'

She reminds me that it was her dad's haunt after the family split up in the 1950s. It is of course also George Kenney's local in *Her Father's Sins*, and in the 1991-'92 *Outcast* trilogy (*Outcast, Alley Urchin* and *Vagabonds*), set in the second half of the 19th century, the pub is a haven for pickpockets and ruffians, and the place where Sal Tanner mistakes the attentions of a fellow in a spotted scarf for an invitation to bed.

Old Sal, a legend in the area, and by the end of the story 'a limping, bedraggled woman with thin, tousled hair and a kindly face that was ravaged by a rough life and a particular love for "a drop o' the ol' stuff",' was modelled on a woman who used to live down on the banks of the canal in a shed. I recalled for Jo the description of the hut in *Alley Urchin* – situated between the pub and the vicarage, a fact that gives the old girl a measure of contentment. 'All the kids used to go and see her,' Jo told me. 'You'd walk to the pub with her and she'd sit you on the step. And you'd hear all this noise going on in the pub and I used to stand on tiptoes and look through the window, and there was Sal on the counter, dancing, drunk as a lord, showing her knickers to all and sundry. She was wonderful!'

Jo caught precisely this scene in *Outcast*:

Not daring to set foot in such a place, Emma stood on tiptoe in order to look through the windows. Her vision was impaired by the frosted pattern on the glass and the large words which read 'Public Bar' on the first window and 'Snug' on the second. Peering through a small corner below, where there was an area of clear glass, Emma's view was still frustrated by the thick smoke screen and the wall of bodies inside... Suddenly a cackle of laughter erupted from within and as Emma peered through the haze in search of her husband, the unmistakable figure of Sal Tanner rose before her. The next moment, the laughing figure was hoisted on to one of the tables by a bevy of reaching, grasping hands. The music took on a more urgent note and the hands all began clapping as Sal Tanner executed a frenzied dance – showing her pink, grinning gums at one end and her pink, dimpled thighs at the other.

Soon after meeting Jo it becomes apparent just how completely the novels are based on her own personal experience – not just the places, but the people too, though this may be subtly done, so that, for example, Auntie Biddy was in real life a quite different character to the one portrayed in *Her Father's Sins*. Only her name is used. Biddy's fictional character is, in fact, that of the author's mother, Mary Jane, who was the fulcrum of Jo's existence as a child, and in a sense remains so to this day:

'My mother was a lovely person. She was ever so warm, you could never fall out with her. She is Marcia in *Angels Cry Sometimes*, and I keep her alive in each new novel. She's always there, sometimes she's an old woman, sometimes a young man... I had to keep her alive, you see. Molly Davidson was also my mother [*Cradle of Thorns*], Marcia is most like her, but she appears in every novel. She could be an old man, a young woman, a little boy – the *persona*, the soul of that character is my mother. My readers are beginning to guess. "*That* is your mother!" In fact, reading the book I am writing now [*The Woman Who Left*], they might think that the female character, Georgie, is my mother, but they'll be fooled if they do, because it is someone who comes into the story later on...'

It was Jo's mum who encouraged her to realise her ambition to become a writer, when the prospect seemed absurd. 'Sadly I didn't have success with the novels when she was alive, but

The character of Sal Tanner was modelled on that of a woman who used to live down on the banks of the canal in a shed. 'All the kids used to go and see her,' Jo recalls.

The Navigation hasn't changed at all. 'It's so old,' says Jo, 'and it's got the wooden benches around the wall and the real old characters, and my god you pick up some tales.'

she's up there, she knows...'

When I ask Jo what she particularly remembers about her mum, it is the simple things, how well they got on, the special, private, one-to-one moments of spontaneous laughter. Any one of the stories she tells me is typical: 'I remember once we were in the scullery and me mam said to me, "Take the potato peelings out of that water in that bowl, put them in the bucket there and swill the yard with the water." You had to go down a flight of steps to the back yard and as you came off the steps at the bottom you'd go into the smallest cellar, where the toilet was, and all the coal was kept in there. After telling me to do this, she went out, and I didn't know where she'd gone. So, anyway, I did what she said, took the potato peelings out of the bowl and put them in the bucket – we used to give them to the milkman who'd take them to the farm to feed to the pigs. Then I took the bowl of water and opened the back door and stood at the top of the steps and I just threw it. At that precise moment me mam came out of the toilet cellar and it went all over her! I thought I'd killed her! I cried my eyes out, and then of course we just laughed and laughed together. Just things like that, *so* lovely.'

Mary Jane had ten children altogether, and, like Amy

Tattersall with her brood in *Looking Back*, the family suffered the trials of so many growing up in a cramped house. 'At one stage we slept six in a bed, three top, three bottom,' Jo recalls, 'You'd get someone's foot in your mouth when you were half asleep. But it was part of the normality of life and there were times when, instead of having blankets, which cost money, you'd have your dad's overcoat over you.

'The house was heated by a coal fire, if you were lucky to have any coal. There was a tiny scullery, no bigger than a few feet. Back parlour, front parlour, each of the parlours had a tiny fire grate.' The scullery appears in *Take This Woman* – 'a cold forbidding place, separated from the parlour by a heavy brown curtain at the door-way. It was some eight feet square, consisting of an old gas-cooker, a single wooden cupboard with several shelves above it, and a deep stone sink beneath the window. Built into the corner was a brick container, housing a copper washtub and closed at the top by a large circular lid of wooden slatted design.'

As the mill-worker colonies got going, schools, churches and the odd hospital were also sponsored by the mill owners. In the building of churches, Roman Catholics benefited least from their largess, as these, often Irish, communities tended to provide the unskilled, labouring class of worker, no less needful of the masters' paternalism, but less significant in the long run to the smooth running of their mills. Jo's dad worked for the council, sweeping the roads.

'He had these beautiful blue eyes and he was fair haired, this little man, and I loved him very much, we all did, but things got a bit difficult when the marriage began to crumble... He worked for the Corporation, various jobs,' Jo tells me. 'He kept Blackburn Rovers football ground, which he was immensely proud of, he kept the roads, maintenance jobs, everything. He was fanatical about Blackburn Rovers. Oh, my dad and my brothers were fanatical. And I loved it. I used to play football in the street and I've got a scar to prove it! See that scar? I dived for the ball and slit my left hand on some glass.'

When Barney, as Jo's dad was called, first met Mary Jane, he was working in the quarries, and she was lodging with her parents (remembered as Grandpa and Grandma Fletcher in *Angels Cry Sometimes)* in Henry Street, Church, a suburb of nearby Accrington. Together Mary Jane and Barney moved to Blackburn, to Derwent Street on the north side of King Street, in the early 1930s.

Still fields in 1822, as the map of that date shows, the area had become a dense concentration of mill workers' terraced rows in the second half of the 19th century, a very poor area, all to be torn down in the 1960s. Ruby Miller lives there in *Nobody's Darling*. Mollie Tattersall and her fiancé, Alfie, try for a house there in *Looking Back*. In *Rainbow Days*, 'the ruined house at the bottom of Derwent

The map, right, shows the area of Derwent Street as it was when Jo was born. Off the map to the north, beyond Preston New Road, lies Corporation Park. To the east lies the market, the station and Cicely Bridge Mill (all of which can be seen on the map on page 55, being closer to Henry Street, to which Jo moved when she was 8). The map here shows the immediate vicinity of Derwent Street, including St Anne's School, which Jo attended. Montague Street cuts diagonally across the map from Preston New Road to King Street in the bottom right-hand corner, where also Bent Street can be seen, still site of the Ragged School today. Addison Street, which figures as Johnson Street in Somewhere, Someday, *leads northwest from the west end of Derwent Street.*

Comparing it with the 1822 map on page 17 is interesting. Clearly the whole site west of Princess (Prince's) Street and north of King Street, which incorporates Derwent Street, has been hugely developed in the intervening years, with mill colonies built much farther north than the 1822 map stretches, close to the hill site of Corporation Park, from where the middle-class housing looked down on them.

Up from Derwent is Greaves Street, which is Oakenhurst Road today. Drop in to the Three Pigeons, where the publican, Rosie Finn, knows all about Jo's dad's favourite pub, the Sun. She was once its landlady. Rosie told me that there were so many pubs in the area that the saying went that if you drank a thimble of alcohol at the nearby Griffin and doubled it at every pub along the way, you would be drunk by the time you got to the Sun at the top of King Street.

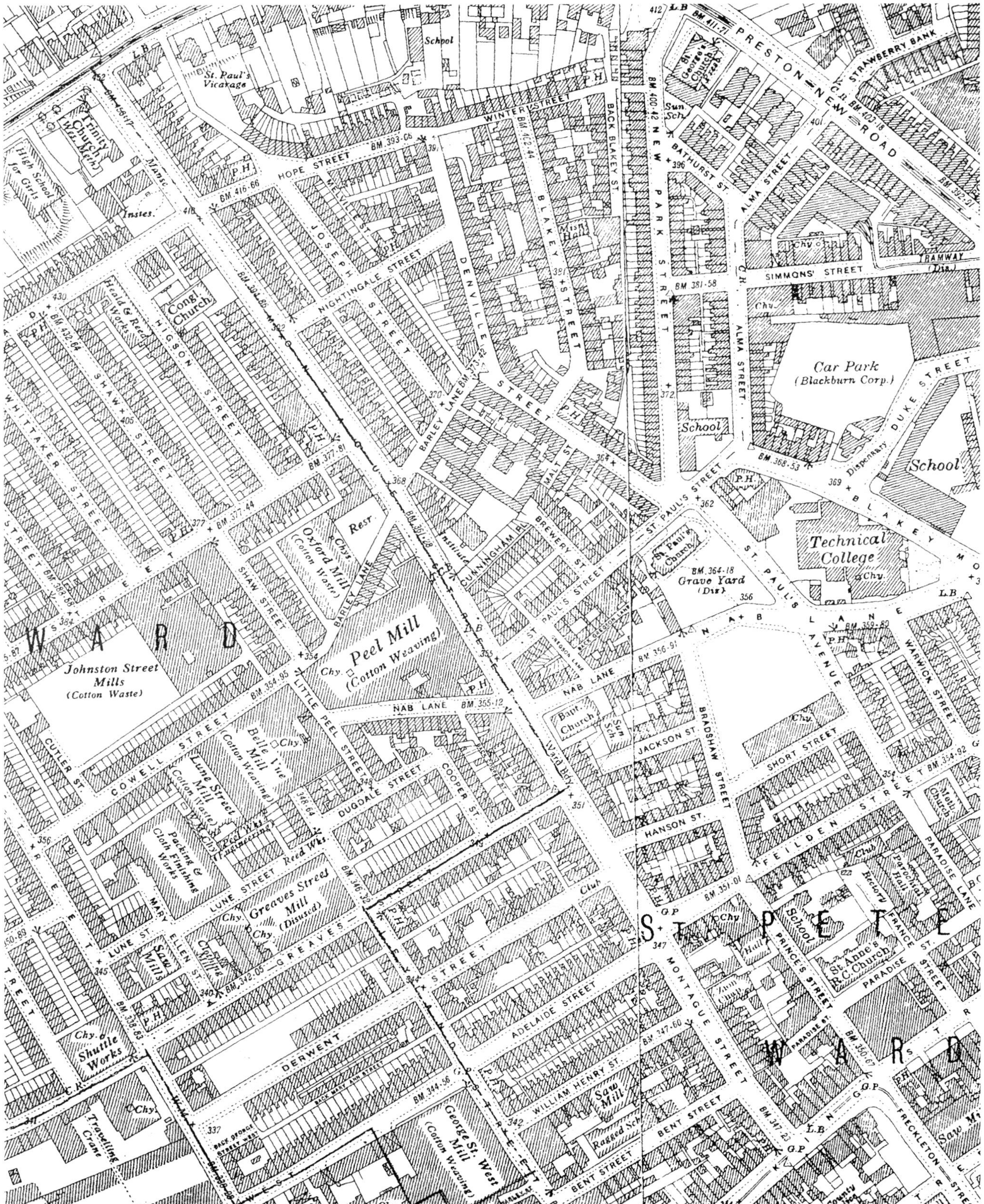

PRESTON NEW ROAD
STRAWBERRY BANK
St. George's Church (Presb.)
School
St. Paul's Vicarage
WINTER STREET
BACK BLAKEY ST.
NEW PARK STREET
BATHURST ST.
ALMA STREET
Trinity Church (Wes. Meth.)
High School for Girls
HOPE STREET
Instes.
JOSEPH STREET
BLAKEY STREET
DENVILLE STREET
Misn. Hall
SIMMONS' STREET
TRAMWAY (Dis.)
NIGHTINGALE STREET
Cong. Church
Heald & Reed Works
HIGSON STREET
SHAW STREET
WHITTAKER STREET
Car Park (Blackburn Corp.)
DUKE STREET
School
BARLEY LANE
MALT ST.
Dispensary
School
BLAKEY MOOR
ST. PAUL'S STREET
Technical College
Oxford Mill (Cotton Waste)
Resr.
Institute
CUNNINGHAM PL.
BREWERY ST.
St. Paul's Church
Grave Yard (Dis.)
ST. PAUL'S AVENUE
NAB LANE
WARWICK STREET
WARD
Johnston Street Mills (Cotton Waste)
Peel Mill (Cotton Weaving)
LITTLE PEEL STREET
Bapt. Church
Sun. Sch.
JACKSON ST.
BRADSHAW STREET
SHORT STREET
CUTLER ST.
COWELL STREET
Belle Vue Mill (Cotton Weaving)
Lune Street Mill (Cotton Waste)
DUGDALE STREET
COOPER ST.
Ward Bdy.
HANSON ST.
FEILDEN STREET
Meth. Church
Club
Rectory
Parochial Hall
PARADISE LANE
Packing & Cloth Finishing Works
Peel Wks. (Engineering)
Reed Wks.
LUNE STREET
MARY ELLEN ST.
Greaves Street Mill (Disused)
GREAVES STREET
ST. PETER
School
Hall
PRINCE'S STREET
St. Anne's R.C. Church
FRANCE STREET
PARADISE ST.
MONTAGUE STREET
Saw Mills
Clothing Works
ADELAIDE STREET
WILLIAM HENRY ST.
DERWENT STREET
BACK MARY ANN STREET
Shuttle Works
Travelling Crane
Saw Mill
Ragged Sch.
BENT STREET
George St. West Mill (Cotton Weaving)
BACK GEORGE STREET WEST
WARD
FRECKLETON STREET
KING STREET
County Court

King Street in the 1940s, near where Jo was born. 'In this area of King Street, where houses lined the street and rows of chimneys pumped dark, foul smoke into the air, there was little room for beauty.' Tomorrow The World

Street was a favourite meeting place for villains.' But in reality, as Jo told me, 'Derwent Street, where we lived, was a real community.'

In between having her many children, and right through her pregnancies, Jo's mum worked in the carding room of Cicely Bridge Mill, preparing the cotton fibres for spinning. Tucked behind the railway station on the south bank of the Leeds-Liverpool canal, Cicely Bridge Mill specialised in spinning, while opposite, Alma Mill specialised in weaving.

Each working day was heralded by the sharp, 5 am rat-a-tat of the knocker-up's stick against the windows of the house in Derwent Street – 'The knocker-up used to wake me dad up to go to work, used to wake the whole house up, actually,' recalls Jo. 'It was a long stick knocking on the windows, still going on in the early 1950s. Every day started the same noisy, predictable way, bleary-eyed workers tumbling from their beds, the screech of the factory hooters, droves of blue overalls, flat caps and khaki demob-coats,

Montague Street, 1950. Jo was born when the family lived in the maze of streets on the left of this picture, see map on page 27.

'Fanny lived right at the top of Montague Street, on the right-hand side, just before the Preston New Road. It was pleasant, long and steep, with wide pavements and houses with big bay windows; on the corner was a warehouse where the rag-and-bone man kept his goods, and after that a row of curious little shops.'
Tomorrow The World

billy-cans a-rattling and snap-tins shaping their deep pockets. And every evening, after a long, back-breaking day, these same workers would laugh and sing in the pubs, which held pride of place in every lamp-lined cobbled street.' In *Angels Cry Sometimes*, Marcia Bendall is Jo's mum, Mary Jane:

The tram shuddered to a halt, jerking Marcia's wandering thoughts to the long hard day ahead at the spinning frames. The bleary-eyed workers, tired and worn even before they started, tumbled from the tram, all pushing and shoving towards their place of labour. 'Morning Marcia lass...' 'Bit parky, eh...shouldn't send a dog out this time o' the day!' 'Ow do, Marcia love; weekend coming up, eh... thank Christ!'

The muffled-up workers shouted their cheery greetings, as they hunched their shoulders against the piercing cold, and set about trudging their way up Cicely to the sprawling cluster of cotton mills there. Marcia returned their friendly greeting with genuine affection...

Cicely Bridge Mill, where Jo's mum worked.

As the hurrying throng of mill-hands swarmed across the top of Cicely Hill to disperse along various paths leading to their respective mills, the sounds of their departing voices was effectively silenced beneath the banshee wail of the five-minute hooter.

'Come on Marcia! You shoulda done your dreaming while you were still abed! Or wouldn't the old fella let you, eh?'

Marcia turned at the coarse laughter which cut through her private thoughts. 'Oh, morning Old Fred,' she said as she stopped for the merest second to rub her hands in the intensity of heat radiating from the brazier. Old Fred was the night-watchman, a harmless little man with a mountain of cheek and more than his fair share of smutty humour...

Jo remembers old Fred very well: 'Harmless, but incredibly ugly. Whenever I went up to Cicely Bridge, he was the little man always sitting there – 'All right lass?' he'd ask. He didn't talk a lot in fact, he was just a funny little creature sitting there.

The view looking back over Cicely Bridge to Blackburn: 'Skirting the busier part of town, Laura took the way past the clutch of cotton mills that stood high on Cicely Banks and looked down over Blackburn town.' Take This Woman

Below: *Each working day was heralded by the sharp, 5 am rat-a-tat of the knocker-up's stick against the windows of the house in Derwent Street – 'The knocker-up used to wake me dad up to go to work, used to wake the whole house up... It was a long stick, knocking on the windows, still going on in the early 1950s.'*

'I remember going in to the mill for the first time and I couldn't believe how hard me mam had to work. They all wore aprons with big pockets. The noise was horrendous! Huge machines, great big rooms.

'And do you know they had their own language? They couldn't hear what was being said, so they had their own language. It wasn't a sign language with fingers but with the mouth. They used their mouths. My mum could talk to someone right at the other end, and they could converse, they knew what each of them was saying. You couldn't hear a thing.'

The most crippling discomfort, and the hardest to get used to, was the noise. The constant high-pitched whine from the machines, tempered with a rhythmic thumping, was painfully deafening and nerve-jarring. In the monstrous Victorian building which swallowed Marcia's days, the spinning and weaving machines dominated thought and action. It was physically impossible for the workers to converse in an easy normal manner. Pitching the mere human voice against the brawling of these tireless machines was utterly futile. So, in the deviousness born of necessity, the Lancashire mill-hands had devised a silent but functional language of their own. With their sophisticated sign and lip-reading language they cheated the screaming machines which sought to render them mute.

Marcia's clocking-in card was the last in the rack. Everyone had punched their cards and placed them in the in-shelves. She slipped the yellow card into the slot over the time-clock, just as the hand swung round to register six a.m. 'Good,' she whispered, tapping the clock gratefully, 'just in time!'

As she pushed against the heavy green doors leading into the cloak-room, she could hear the machines starting up one after the other. Wriggling

Tucked behind the railway station on the south bank of the Leeds-Liverpool canal, Cicely Bridge Mill, where Jo's mum worked, specialised in spinning. 'Often, at the end of the day, I would walk up to Cicely Bridge and meet me mam,' Jo remembers. 'I pushed the little babbies in the pram to meet her. I was only about nine meself. I would sit waiting for her, sit on a stool at the bottom of the run.'

out of her coat, she slung it hurriedly over one of the pegs on the rack before hastening to her own machine.

'Come on Marcia! Where the 'ell 'ave you been?' Tom Atkinson was the gaffer. A great elephant of a man he was; shaped like one of the cotton-bobbins, swollen to bulging in the middle and tapered off at both ends. His watery red-rimmed eyes were incapable of direct focus because while the left one struggled to hold you tight in its quivering gaze, the right one swivelled about all over the place, until finally out of utter frustration the pair of them gave up the effort...

Without uncovering her long black hair, she skilfully manipulated the scarf about her head, transforming it into a knotted turban which sat tight and snug, concealing and protecting her magnificent hair from the clinging wisps of cotton which would soon fill the air like sticky snowflakes. Reaching into a small wooden locker beneath her bobbin-crate, she exchanged her ankle-clogs for soft slippers. Then she donned the regular green wrap-around overall. Strapping the deep-pocketed pinny around her waist, and checking the bottom tray-run to assure herself that it was filled all the way along with empty bobbins, Marcia threw the machine into gear. Marcia wasn't normally given to nervousness, but the act of triggering the monstrous machine into life was definitely not one in which she took pleasure.

'Often, at the end of the day, I would walk up to Cicely Bridge and meet me mam,' Jo remembers. 'I pushed the little babbies in the pram to meet her. I was only about nine meself. I would sit waiting for her, sit on a stool at the bottom of the run. I can see her now, at

Mill women in the 1930s, some shawled and clogged in traditional style.

'"Come on Marcia! You shoulda done your dreaming while you were still abed! Or wouldn't the old fella let you, eh?" Marcia turned at the coarse laughter which cut through her private thoughts.' Angels Cry Sometimes

the end of each run of machine they would have a box and they would keep their slippers in there and these slippers were the funniest thing because they were just big clumps like of snow, where all the cotton had settled on them, month after month. The cotton, it would fall like snow and you'd be covered in it in five seconds, and the slippers just grew, and they shoved their feet into these great things and ran up and down. She had eight bobbins to look after...'

These bobbins received the carded fibres – a slender rope or 'roving' of spun cotton fibres – which would wind round the bobbin in preparation for weaving.

'She had to keep putting the empty bobbins on and taking the full ones off, dropping them in her apron. And if you weren't quick then it'd spill over and you'd be in a dreadful mess.

'Tom Atkinson, the gaffer. I remember him. He was a man of few words, in charge of my mother's section. He didn't like children.

He didn't speak to me. He was just someone that was there who was part of what was going on in my mother's life, you know?

'But Big Bertha was the woman who worked on the next lot of machines from my mum. The one thing I remember about her was that she had this big round face and was always laughin'! And they were always running up and down. It seems really strange to think of it now... They worked like this from six in the morning till six at night.

The machines were an awesome sight to behold. The great iron monsters, proud and domineering, reached endlessly upwards and outwards measuring in excess of sixty feet, and seeming as tall again. Almost touching the towering Victorian ceilings, they blotted out both light and human sound. Hundreds of bobbins spanned each machine, swirling and screeching beneath the weight of spinning cotton.

It was incredible to the watching eye that such heinous constructions could belch forth a cotton as fine and pure as the beautiful delicate strands of a cobweb. The cotton poured out in great abundance, winding and wrapping itself around the receptive bobbins which spun and twirled, until swollen pregnantly with their heavy load. When full, the heavy bobbins would be removed by the harassed scurrying women who constantly raced against time and machine as they darted methodically from one end of the heaving row to the other, their coloured turbans making frenzied patterns as they wove up and down, up and down.

The frequent replacement of empty bobbins for full ones was swift and skilful. The empty bobbins were quickly dropped with great accuracy over the fast spinning core-rods. It took only a few minutes for the empty bobbins to fill to bursting again; allowing the constantly mobile women no rest. They were hard pushed to keep up, and many a trainee had surrendered in tears to the devouring machines. The full bobbins were slipped into the hessian bag which the women wore around their waists until the bag reached overflowing. The bobbins were then emptied into large square wicker containers. These, in turn, were emptied into huge mobile trollies, which were frequently transported to another level of the mill by an organised army of 'trundlers'. The fine cotton would then be woven into endless acres of fresh crisp linen, to be shipped all over the world, as well as marketed locally.

'Do you remember the man in the novel who used to take the trolleys and the women scragged him?' Jo asked me. 'Well, my mam told me about this man, Tommy Trindle, who took the full bobbin trolleys away and brought the empty trolleys back and he was always pinching their bottoms and making snide little comments, so they did scrag him one day. They got his trousers off and shoved him down the ramp in the trolley!'

George Leatherhead was a 'trundler' who took a pride in his work... Unfortunately for poor George, some of the young flighty girls, always ready for a bit of fun at the end of a working day, had overheard his brazen remarks. He didn't get very far before they were on him, their pent-up exuberance now released in fits of screaming laughter.

'Right, you sexy beast, George Leatherhead! You've asked for it now!' 'Don't get worriting, George... we're not going to 'arm you... we just want to see what all the fuss is about.' 'Come on George! Get them bloody trousers off!' They came at him from all directions...

Stories like this leave little doubt about the camaraderie that relieved the 12-hour work shifts until the factory hooter blew for shutdown and the spinning machines were wound down. Bit by bit the blanket of noise broke up and dissipated, as one by one the individual sources of it were extinguished. Normally a swell of laughter and chatter would replace the machine noise, but on one occasion, Jo tells me, there was only hushed silence. 'That terrible scene in *Angels Cry Sometimes* is based on something that one of the ladies who worked with mam told me when she took me to the toilet... She was telling me about this girl... and then, "Don't you go near the machines, lass," she said...

'Come on Marcia! Get your apron emptied!' But even as Marcia was lifting her hand to throw the switch which would close down her machine, there came an almighty noise from some way up in front – a great screeching,

Two weavers, 25 and 17 years of age, in the 1930s: "Right, you sexy beast, George Leatherhead! You've asked for it now!'" "Don't get worriting, George... we're not going to 'arm you... we just want to see what all the fuss is about.'" "Come on George! Get them bloody trousers off!'" They came at him from all directions...'
Angels Cry Sometimes

jarring noise, which was unlike anything she'd beard before. Then, of a sudden, it was like all hell let loose! Folks ran in all directions and even Tom Atkinson, who judging by the heightened colour of his face and the wild look in his eyes, could go down any minute with a heart-attack, pelted past Marcia's machine.

By now most of the machines had ground to a halt. But, when Marcia emerged from changing her slippers for shoes, she saw little groups of mill-hands standing about and conversing in whispers. From a distance, she could see Daisy crying, with old Bertha comforting her. Some of the other women were stark-eyed, with their hands flattened over their mouths as though to stifle any sound that might come out.

Going to where old Bertha had young Daisy enclosed in her arms, Marcia asked in a soft voice, subdued by the sight of wretched faces all about her, 'What is it, Bertha? Whatever's going on?'

But Bertha could give no answer, except to shake her head and gently

When the factory hooter blew for shutdown and the spinning machines wound down, bit by bit the blanket of noise broke up and dissipated.

'Hordes of cotton mill workers huddled together... their flat caps like a sea of twill and their snap-cans clinking in rhythm with the stamp of their iron-rimmed clogs on the pavements. The streets were alive with the sounds...'

Jessica's Girl

to lead away the trembling girl in her arms. As she passed Marcia she whispered, 'Come away, lass. Come away!' As Marcia made to follow her... there came a flurry of activity from both behind and in front of her.

Tom Atkinson walked about, going from one little group to another, gently moving them on and telling them, 'Tek yersels off home. There's nowt to be done 'ere!' His face looked totally drained of colour and his shoulders stooped as though pressed down with a great weight.

When the two dark-suited fellows came hurrying by her carrying a rolled-up stretcher and looking grim, Marcia's eyes followed them and, almost involuntarily, she took a few paces forward. What she saw came as one of the worst shocks she had ever experienced. It was Maggie Clegg's machine around which all activity was taking place – bright chirpy Maggie Clegg's machine, splattered from top to bottom in great splashes of blood standing out scarlet and horrifying against the white cotton bobbins and the great iron struts, which Maggie knew like the back of her hand. From the huge cogs and rollers which ran this monstrosity, there hung ragged hanks of hair – Maggie's hair that was once long and jet-black, and which now was crimson and split asunder.

The Weave of Life

People relate to Jo's books because her fictional world is ground out of the world that she knew so well in the first fourteen years of her life. It was sometimes a harsh reality, but characterful and seamless. In the novels, as in life, character is not distinct from environment, it *is* environment, so that, for example, Queenie's home draws from Auntie Biddy's strong, loving character:

'It was a little house we had in Derwent Street,' Jo recalls, 'they were all little houses, but it was a real community.'

There was a degree of warmth and splendid reliability in the stalwart green distemper, which reflected the half-light from the gas-lamp beneath the window. The big square wardrobe stood to attention in its disciplined uprightness, as it towered protectively over a short wooden-knobbed chest of drawers. A small ripple of pleasure bathed the knot of fear in Queenie's stomach as her gaze rested on the kidney-shaped dresser... There in the half-light were all the familiar things.

'It was a little house we had in Derwent Street,' Jo recalls, 'they were all little houses, but it was a real community. You could go out and leave your door unlocked, then come back and find six people sitting in your kitchen drinking tea. The women all looked after each other's children. Nobody had much, but we shared what we had. From Derwent Street come the really early memories, when I was four, five years old and I would sit on the step and watch everything as it was going on in the street.' There were other more or less permanent sentinels, too, like old Mr Craig from No. 46 –

Queenie liked Mr Craig, who spent long lonely days sitting outside his little house. The rickety stand-chair had a permanent place on the flagstones by the front door. Folks had long ago stopped asking questions or wondering why it was that a stand-chair should be left outside in all weathers year in year out. They'd gotten used to the old fellow sitting there, happy to pass the time of day with anyone who could spare it. From early morning to last thing at night when the biting chill of evening forced him in, he'd just sit there smiling and chatting to one and all, and generally watching the world go by.

During her flag-counting sessions, Queenie would often run errands for him, or come and set herself on his step, where she'd listen enthralled to exciting stories of his daredevil days and frightening accounts of the war he'd fought in as a young man.

'All the children would follow him up and down the street as if he was the Pied Piper. And then he was arrested one day.'

The working class community of Derwent Street comes to us in the novels as a woven tapestry of relationships, the idiosyncratic ways of Jo's characters so often proving them true. 'I remember Derwent Street in particular because we had a chap who used to live at the top end, who dressed up in high heels and short skirts! All the children would follow him up and down the street as if he was the Pied Piper. And then he was arrested one day. The policemen were taking him off and we were all running after him! We all loved him! He was so kind, a lovely man.'

In *Her Father's Sins*, he appears in the guise of Fountain Crossland, 'who had fists the size of sledge-hammers and a head like a stud-bull, a burly pitworker,' but who would rather be wearing Auntie Biddy's pinny and dandling Queenie on his knee.

It was a pleasing picture that greeted Fountain Crossland when George Kenney's daughter opened the door to his tapping. 'A sight for sore eyes, that's what you are, young Queenie,' he said quietly. Then without waiting to be asked he stepped inside and proceeded down the passageway towards the parlour. Queenie closed the door and followed. 'He's still in bed,' she said, leaving the parlour door open as she came in from the passage. 'No need fer that,' Fountain Crossland told her, his face crooked into a half-smile.

Queenie had already turned away with the intention of rousing George Kenney but now the big man came to block her exit. Putting his finger across his lips he leaned towards her, at the same time reaching out behind her to push the door to. 'Ssh . . . we don't want to fetch 'im from 'is bed, do we? I've seen what 'es like on wakkening!' He stretched his face into an ugly grimace, and it was such an accurate mimicry of George Kenney in a foul temper that Queenie found herself laughing out loud in spite of herself. Auntie Biddy had no liking for Fountain Crossland, Queenie knew, but he could be so funny, and a great deal nicer than George Kenney.

'Auntie Biddy abed too is she?'

'Yes . . . she's been badly.'

'Ah! Works too 'ard does Biddy.' Fountain Crossland seated himself in the horse-chair by the fireside, all the while regarding Queenie through careful eyes. 'I'll tell you what, lass,' he said quietly, 'let's you an' me 'ave a little talk eh?' His broad smile was disarming, and when he stretched out a hand Queenie went to him.

At once he pulled her on to his knee and Queenie was quickly enthralled by the stories he told her . . . funny stories about little creatures who lived in folks' mattresses and who had the most marvellous adventures.

It seemed that Fountain Crossland got carried away in excitement, because once or twice Queenie found herself being violently jiggled up and down on his lap. And when at one stage Fountain Crossland took to acting out a scene where he took off his trousers and put on Auntie Biddy's pinafore he looked so silly that Queenie fell about laughing.

It was this scene that Auntie Biddy came upon when she brought herself down from the bedroom to investigate the noise. It took her but a moment to see Fountain Crossland's real game and with a cry of 'You fornicating old sod!' she grabbed up his trouser belt and whacked it hard across his bare legs. 'Out! Get out and don't show yourself here again!' she told him. Even when Fountain Crossland took to his heels and ran off up the passage without his trousers, Auntie Biddy would have followed him if it hadn't been for that fact that the bubble of energy she had summoned was now depleted. Falling into the nearest chair, she told the gaping Queenie, 'Throw 'is old trousers after him, lass.'

This Queenie did, firmly closing the front door after both Fountain Crossland and his trousers had disappeared through it, only to be tripped head over heels by Mrs Farraday's terrified ginger tom. When she returned to the parlour, Queenie was uncertain as to whether she would be blamed for letting Fountain Crossland into the house, and looked into the little woman's face with a sheepish expression.

'I'm sorry, Auntie Biddy,' Queenie said. For a moment there came no response. Then, just as Queenie began to think she would not be forgiven, she noticed a twinkle which spread into a smile and the smile erupted into laughter. Queenie ran to her Auntie Biddy and together the two of them rocked helplessly at the memory of Fountain Crossland fleeing up the passage in a pinny, after having his buttocks well and truly thrashed by Auntie Biddy.

Time and again it is the women who are the strongest characters. 'The women of Lancashire were a race unto themselves,' Jo has written.

'You have to love life, and love people if you are going to write stories,' says Jo today. 'You must live the part of every character, even the bad ones. When I am writing I am laughing and crying, and feeling angry and sad. I have so many stories I would have to live to 200 to write them all.'

Time and again it is Jo's women who make the strongest characters, which is not the same as saying that she draws them better than her men. 'The women of Lancashire were a race unto themselves,' Jo has written. 'They experienced few luxuries, accepting hard work and domineering husbands as part of their unenviable lot.

'Now, Ada Humble in *Angels Cry Sometimes* was my mam's friend. She was. a fat little woman, a lovely, lovely person.' Ada is noted for her washing line and 'the numerous shirt-tails that pranced in the drying breeze, telling the world and its neighbour that she was the proud custodian of seven darling men.'

The novels are littered with imaginative observations from the perspective of the curious little girl next door – like Mr Eddies' long-johns 'squirming half in half out' of Biddy's mangle, or Mrs Aspen's gossip box, used to stand on so that she can chit-chat across the back-yard wall. Most significant, however, was Ada's red trilby.

'She had a red trilby, and, do you know, she wore that trilby everywhere. She lived next door to us, and we would laugh when every morning she would come out and bend down to pick up the milk and her trilby would stay on! She never would be seen without that trilby. What happened to Ada was very sad. She had five sons. One of them wouldn't go to school. She used to come and tell my mam, and my mam said, "Take him in. Put him through the door. Make sure he gets into the classroom." Ada did this, but he would still run off and the truant officer kept coming round, and finally he said, "If the boy doesn't go to school, you'll have to go to Court." Ada was taken to Court. My mam went with her. Poor thing, she was jailed, for six months! They decreed that Ada's husband [Toby] couldn't be blamed because he had been at work – it was the mother at home's fault, so Ada was put in jail. When she came out she was broken! She had lost all her weight – she was like a stick – she was white, she was haggard and she died soon after. It was terrible.

'Now, when somebody died, all the people in the street had to go along and pay their respects, and the children too. I said, "No." I didn't want to go. And I kicked and screamed. But my mam dragged us along, and there was little Ada in her coffin without her hat, and she was completely bald. That was why she had always worn the trilby! None of us had known. My mother saw the hat on the chair and she picked it up and put it on Ada's head. I'll never forget that.'

The inhabitants of the old terraced houses were as varied and interesting as the higgledy-piggledy houses themselves, like Martha Heigh –

She could be seen now, standing on her doorstep, stretching her neck so as not to miss anything. Martha Heigh, never bothered to wash... or so it was told. Anyone, it was rumoured, with even half a nose could not bear to stand within range of the very nasty aroma which constantly surrounded old Martha.

She'd lived on her own in the last house along the row these thirty-odd years, since the death of her poor old father. Nobody knew her real age although folks reckoned it to be grander than eighty. She rarely ventured from the safety of her home, and the only person she had ever allowed inside it was Marcia who, to the horror of her neighbours, often fetched groceries for the old woman.

Martha was as short and round as a little Toby jug, and the full-length skirts she wore did nothing to enhance her appearance. More often than not, the skirt was employed as a convenient dish rag. She'd wipe her hands on it, blow her snuffy brown nostrils on it... she was using it now to shine up her precious tiny silver spectacles, which were then promptly placed on her nose with delicate precision as she peered to focus.

Her hair stood out in a petrified state of attention and the nervous nodding habit she'd cultivated accelerated with excitement at the appearance of the new neighbours. The wide appreciative grin as she suddenly saw Marcia displayed the blackened rows of teeth; of the naturalness of which she was duly proud. Marcia smiled back, waving her hand in acknowledgement.

Sometimes Jo allows characters to earn a place in her street, even though they actually lived elsewhere in the town. Two elderly sisters, Edith and Sarah Atkinson, were supposed to have occupied the house next door to Jo for many years and to be long sufferers of the Humble family, 'whom Edith described as "too bloody noisy by half!"' In fact, they were modelled on Jo's Auntie Betty and her friend. 'We went past the house the other week,' Jo told me. 'It is still there. It's on the Accrington Road and it backs on to the canal. The canal is down low and the window to the parlour is high, it's quite a drop. When my Auntie Betty wasn't looking I used to sit on the window sill with my legs dangling and I remember one day she screamed out – I nearly fell in the water when she screamed! – and grabbed hold of me, yanking me back. After that I couldn't open the window. I don't know what she did, she must have put nails in or something. That was my Auntie Betty. I never did know her friend's name.'

'Owd Chipper', a spinner by trade and later a rag and bone man (real name Robert Reynolds), with his peep show (old war pictures of the Boer War and tin soldiers), with which he amused Blackburn children from around 1900.

Never mind, she, like Betty, is preserved for posterity in *Angels Cry Sometimes*:

Sarah Atkinson, at seventy-two, was the younger by six years. She was a tiny, shrivelled figure with pretty brown hair and a shawl to match; she was partially deaf and completely blind. The older one, Edith, was a huge hulk of a woman, grossly obese and extremely ugly. Her startling white hair was always piled high up into an untidy fat bun. Marcia had only ever seen Edith Atkinson's hair down once, when she wasn't surprised to see it reaching way past the old woman's thick waist. Edith's nasty narrow eyes missed nothing, and she constantly bullied her handicapped sister, ruling her with a merciless rod of iron. It was rumoured that they were 'worth a few bob' since the demise of the last of their relatives.

Then there were the street traders – the peddler, the tinker with pots and pans, the scissors grinder and the barrel organ grinder:

A little wizened man had placed his barrel organ in a shrewd position, so that anyone emerging from Ainsworth Street had no choice but to pass him before reaching the centre of activity.

'Good evening one an' all!' His voice was an odd grating squeak which seemed to suit his tiny size and general set-up. Fascinated at both his goblin-like appearance and whole unusual ensemble before them, the little

'"Good evening one an' all!" His voice was an odd grating squeak which seemed to suit his tiny size and general set-up. Fascinated at both his goblin-like appearance and whole unusual ensemble before them, the little party ground to a halt.'

Young 'uns, who spent their days sitting on the kerbs with sugar butties; sailing matchstick boats down the gutters; and dropping loose stones into the stinking drains.

party ground to a halt.

'Mam! Just look at that!' Polly's voice was tremulous with the eager excitement of a child, 'That's a monkey!' The incredulity in Polly's voice caused them to stare all the harder.

'That's right lass. You're looking at the gamest little monkey in Lancashire!' The wizened man stepped forward with the monkey squatting skilfully on the bony protrusion of his shoulder and the light from a corner street-lamp illuminated the weird pair. Marcia couldn't help but notice the striking resemblance between the monkey and its shrunken owner. They were both of the same scrawny appearance, and even the cheeky red cap perched jauntily on the monkey's head was identical to the one worn by the man. 'I'm tellin' you,' he continued to squawk, 'there's no monkey in the whole of Lancashire – perhaps the whole world – as can do tricks like my Jasper 'ere!' He swung the monkey by the length of its confining lead to land with a soft thud on Polly's shoulder. His quick jerky movements startled her into springing forward, whereupon the monkey flew into the air, emitting a series of jabbering squawks and chatters, before landing squarely on the side of the barrel-organ.

Pre-eminent among the street traders was, of course, the rag-and-bone merchant. *Take This Woman*, set in Blackburn in 1947, presents us with Laura Blake, who makes a canny living out of 'tatting', as it is known. She collected from a lumbering wooden cart, manoeuvring it by settling herself between its long curved shafts, and taking a firm grip with each hand. She'd collect from the smart area of town, along the Preston New Road, and then wend her way back towards Remmie Thorpe's rag-and-bone shop, where she might exchange some of what she had collected for a few shillings. But Laura found a better welcome in her own part of town, as this extract shows:

The women, all turbanned, laughing or talking, and nearly all pregnant, were busy white-stoning the steps, washing the windows, or watching young 'uns, who spent their days sitting on the kerbs with sugar butties; sailing matchstick boats down the gutters; and dropping loose stones into the stinking drains.

'Hey up!' Smiling Tilly Shiner was the first to spot Laura and her cumbersome cart. 'It's young Laura!'

'Tongue 'anging out for a brew, I expect.' The broad-faced Belle Strong waved a fat dimpled arm towards Laura. 'Get your arse into my kitchen, young 'un!' she shouted coarsely, her numerous chins waggling and bright round eyes laughing. 'Leave yon cart agin the kerb. They'll 'ave it filled in no time, lass!'

And what does Tilly intend to give her? A pair of brown, iron-clad clogs. In *Her Father's Sins*, Jo recalls the occasion when, as a youngster, she took her dad's boots out to another rag-and-bone lady. Maisie Thorogood was as much part of the street scene 'as the gas-lamps and the shiny worn cobblestones. In real life she was really quite

Cotton kids, 1948. 'They had grown up together...living in each other's houses, playing on the cobblestones and scouring the marketplace after closing in search of good pickings.' Jessica's Girl

bad, which was why I called her Thoro*good* in the book.' In the continuation of Queenie's story, *Let Loose The Tigers*, Maisie and her daughter, Sheila, are charged with keeping an immoral house in Lytham St Anne's, and Sheila is sent to prison for five years. In real life, Maisie's great weakness concerned the Yanks. The American GIs came to the town in 1944. They arrived to prepare for the invasion of Europe and were accommodated in the then disused Brookhouse Mill. 'Maisie liked them a lot,' Jo's mother had informed her, 'and when the Yanks left, she was left behind with twins, called Raymond and Sheila in the book. I grew up with them.

'Maisie had connections with everything. She was amazing.

'A small army of excited children queued with their armfuls of odd artefacts: holey kettles, old lead-pipe, and anything else that might entreat Maisie to part with a yo-yo or a bright floating balloon.'

She was wonderful! She was like fairyland! She had this cart that she had painted, and she attached balloons to it. You thought the whole thing was going to take off! You couldn't miss her. Big peroxide blond hair. A voice like a sergeant major. Great sense of humour. She'd have everyone in stitches. The men used to tease her and torment her and she'd give 'em as good as she got, swore like a trooper –'

Clutching George Kenney's old boots, Queenie hopped and skipped the few flagstones which separated her from the rag-a-bone wagon. Its presence within the excited screeching throng of children was pinpointed by the numerous clusters of waving balloons. Every colour of the rainbow they were, dancing and jiggling towards the sky in erratic fits and starts, as the ticklish breeze played and teased the restraining strings.

There were sausage-shaped ones, round ones, egg-shaped and twisty ones; all wriggling and singing as they rubbed together gleefully. Queenie had often imagined Maisie Thorogood sitting in her parlour blowing up the balloons. The magnitude of such an operation had prompted her on more than one occasion to ask Maisie where she kept all that wind, and if it took her all week to get the balloons ready. Maisie would roll about and scream with laughter. 'Bless your 'eart, Queenie darlin', she'd shout, 'didn't you know I keeps a goblin in me shoe. It's 'im as blows 'em up!' So frustrated and perplexed had Queenie grown at this regular answer that eventually she told Sheila, 'I think your Mam's as daft as a barm-cake!' Sheila had agreed most fervently.

The laughter and squeaky chatter of the delighted children filled the air, bringing the women to their doors to smile appreciatively at Maisie, with her rag-a-bone wagon and her little following army. Queenie muscled her way in, pushing and shoving with such deliberation that the deep barrier of small bodies reluctantly gave way to let her through. Not graciously though, judging by the angry snorts, sly sharp kicks, and loud abuse.

'Give over snotrag! Wait yer turn!'

'Hey! Who do you think you are?'

'Cor! Them bloody boots don't 'arf stink!'

Stink they may have done but Queenie didn't care! Not if that was why they'd all moved aside to let her in, she thought.

Her strong grey eyes widened in amazement as they lit on the appearance of Maisie's wagon!

The spill of bright colour and treasure fair blinded her. The low sides of the wagon were painted in Catherine wheels of gaudy reds, yellows, and blacks; the big wooden-spoked wheels made a body dizzy as the zig-zag lines which wound about them screamed first in gold, then green and ended up in a delightful mingling of black and yellow blobs. The whole wonderful marvellous ensemble was entrancing, The inside of the wagon was filled to bursting and, at the shaft end, where the scabby little donkey tucked noisily into his oversized hay-bag, the piles of old rags and varying artefacts were stacked sky-high.

The remainder of the wagon was loaded down with penny-whistles; bundles of clothes-pegs; goldfish swimming about in little fat plastic bags; big blocks of white stepstone, and small tidy bundles of wood-stick for the fire.

Around the rim of the wagon hung more cherry-red yo-yos than Queenie had ever seen in her life. Handmade they were, as Maisie was quick to point out; and polished as shiny as a still pond. They clattered against the clusters of metal-tipped spinning-tops, which also hung in groups of twenty or more from the crowded rim. Then all along the shaft arms dangled hundreds of coloured soft balls, gleaming and winking as the daylight caught the glinting lashing colours within. Finally, every spare inch of space was taken up by the myriads of brightly coloured balloons; so many that Queenie wondered why the donkey, wagon and all, hadn't been clear lifted off the ground to be swept away forever.

'Right then little Queenie! You've shoved your way affront o' these other brats, so what's it to be, eh?' demanded Maisie.

While Jo can claim that her characters are based on real people, she does change some of their physical attributes, and 'sometimes I put two or three people together to produce a character.' Besides Molly Davidson in *Cradle of Thorns*, who is Jo's mum, there are a number of Mollies in the novels, but in a particular Dedication, Jo refers to a Molly who had known her as an urchin and had watched her grow up and get married. Curious as to who this figure might be, I asked Jo about her. She replied, 'Molly was every woman who looked after the children in the street we were in. She was the epitome of the granny if you like. She'd be in her sixties and she'd be small and round and she'd have a kind face and grey hair and tin curlers...'

Generally, characters are more readily identifiable, such as my personal favourites among the old world characters that Jo fingers in the novels: two fine ladies of mature years, Tilly and Fancy Carruthers. 'They were always in bed,' Jo laughs, as she brings them to mind. 'They would have been deemed lesbians today. They lived right up the top in Montague Street. I knew them because I had a friend who lived next door, Sheila Bullen. Poor Sheila, she married a man called King... It was in all the papers – I heard it on the radio – her husband shot her! He shot her while she was holding the baby and the bullet went right through and killed them both. My sister-in-law, Pat, claimed she had gone to see Sheila in her coffin, and she said it broke her heart because the baby was right there, lying at her mother's feet. Sheila was a beautiful girl, long, black, wavy hair, very dark eyes. She was my friend, I went to school with her. We used to run errands for these two old ladies. So many characters...'

Here are Aunt Biddy and little Queenie returning the ladies' laundry in a well-plotted trip that takes in a number of characters in the vicinity of their home, before finally arriving at the Misses Carruthers:

The front door was open into the passage. It was always open. Miss Tilly and Fancy Carruthers loved nothing more than to have visitors. They were always welcome, any time of the day or evening. 'Go and tap on the parlour door, Queenie. Tell 'em we've fetched their washing.'

Queenie skipped along the passage, making the very same bet with herself that she had made on every single occasion: that the two old ladies would both be abed and wearing frilly green caps.

Sure enough, on command of the thin piping voice which urged them to 'come in', the same peculiar scene awaited. The tiny parlour reeked of snuff and something suspiciously like George Kenney [Queenie's dad] when he'd been boozing. The big bed which reached right up to Queenie's shoulders nigh filled the room. The top and bottom of it were like the bars of a jail, and each tall corner was conspicuously marked by huge shiny brass bells, which distorted Queenie's face whenever she looked into them. It would stretch wide and misshapen, then it would squeeze into itself like a concertina, shaping Queenie's mouth into a long narrow 'O', which quickly vanished into her sucked-in-cheeks.

There was real carpet on the floor, and big soft flowery armchairs which could swallow a body whole. Plants reached out from everywhere – from the tiny sideboard, the whatnot, the slipper-box, and even from the shelves on the wall.

'Hello Queenie love. Go and fetch your Auntie Biddy – tell her to push the pram down the passage. It'll save her a few steps carrying the washing.'

Queenie had never seen Miss Tilly out of that bed so she wasn't rightly sure what shape she was, or even if there was any more of her than peeped above the

'The cobble-stones in the road were just the same as when his sister and Phoebe had skipped on them, jutting from the ground like shiny wet loaves and worn thinner by the tread of many feet.' Jessica's Girl

bedclothes. But a good guess, calculated by the tiny pointed face sticking out from beneath the green frilly cap, and the small straight shoulders draped over with a pretty white shawl, told Queenie she was probably right little. Her eyes, though, were huge. Bright blue and stary, with long ginger lashes which looked as though they did not belong to the smiling wizened face.

Sitting next to her, as always, was Fancy Carruthers, nodding and agreeing with everything Miss Tilly said. 'That's right dear,' she kept saying, 'that's right.' Her features were very grey and wrinkled, and her eyes had sunk away into deep bony caves, which prompted Queenie's silent comparison of her to a skeleton. From the brow of her frilly green cap a strand of thick grey hair hung down the wrinkled forehead. Queenie liked them both. She didn't fully understand their strange goings-on, but she liked them well enough.

It was hard, though, for Queenie to reckon on how it was that the teapot, on the firebrick in the hearth, always contained a hot brew; and the cake-tin on the sideboard was never empty of delicious home-made cakes. They must get out of bed sometimes, she reasoned. But t'was an odd thing, a very odd thing!

'Climb up here, young 'un. Let's get a closer look at you.' Miss Tilly

Just as Maisie Thorogood was 'as much part of the street scene as the gas-lamps and the shiny worn cobblestones', so Jo and her friends were at one with the place, playing in the maze of streets unfettered by parental control, like fauns in some lantern-lit, urban Narnia.

patted the bolster beside her. 'Yes, climb up, young Queenie.' Fancy Carruthers screwed her face into a peculiar shape of concentration as she seconded Miss Tilly's request.

Queenie looked around at Auntie Biddy, as if to seek her approval. Upon receipt of Auntie Biddy's reassuring smile, she proceeded to hoist herself up on to the cream-coloured eiderdown. It was no easy task, for the bed was high and the soft eiderdown gave way beneath her grasping fingers.

'Come on,' Miss Tilly encouraged.

'Yes, come on,' repeated Fancy Carruthers. Finally, Queenie clasped both her hands round the big brass ball and climbed up along the top. Scrabbling to where Miss Tilly had indicated, she felt as though she'd just climbed a mountain. Sinking into the squashy depths of the bolster, she looked hard into Miss Tilly's eyes, and waited politely.

Miss Tilly grabbed her by the hand, squeezing it affectionately. 'Been helping your Auntie Biddy take the pressing round, 'ave you lass?' Her features gathered themselves into a tight pointed smile as she looked down at Auntie Biddy... 'Fair worn out she looks, bless 'er.'

'Yes,' Fancy Carruthers muttered, her head nodding in fervent agreement, 'fair worn out.'

Alas, nothing is forever, and, given the special nature of a child's first feelings, there is terrible poignancy when, much later in the novel, Jo, as Queenie, confronts and contemplates the loss of Fancy:

Miss Tilly was propped up against a bolster. Her huge watery-blue eyes were now drained of the vivacity which Queenie had always admired so, and their size, which had always been considerable, seemed even more prominent in the shrinking folds of her aged face. It struck Queenie that the smile which had

King Street shop fronts, 1940s. 'The council moved us to a tripe shop in King Street. There was a slaughter house behind, it was awful! We didn't use the part of the building that was the shop, fronting the road, but we had all the accommodation behind, and behind that was the river and the slaughterhouse. The smell was absolutely appalling. It wasn't a happy memory there.'

always been perpetual on Miss Tilly's face had developed into a peculiar fixed grimace. A feeling of overpowering helplessness engulfed Queenie as she moved towards the old woman.

Miss Tilly swivelled her enormous eyes upwards to focus squarely on Queenie. 'Hello little 'un,' she piped in an odd shrill voice, lifting a hand for Queenie to grasp, 'Oh, I miss her you know.' She glanced at the pillow beside her, then looked away quickly as though afraid of what she might see. 'Took her away, they did, Queenie, been my darling friend for sixty-odd years...' Her wrinkled mouth lifted ever so carefully at the corners and a big pear-shaped tear fell out of one eye. 'Oh, Queenie lass,' she croaked, ''taint the same no more wi'out her.'

When Jo was about six or seven years of age, they left Derwent Street. It was not a good move: 'We were very poor and constantly moved home. After Derwent Street, the council moved us to a tripe shop in King Street. There was a slaughter house behind, it was awful! We didn't use the part of the building that was the shop, fronting the road, but we had all the accommodation behind, and behind that was the river and the slaughterhouse. The smell was absolutely appalling. It wasn't a happy memory there. Nothing went right. I rescued a red setter there from the dog pound, paid two shillings for him I remember. I worked selling jam jars for those two shillings, and Bernard accidentally let him out onto the road. He went straight under a lorry. No, it wasn't a happy house that one!

'The house had a cellar, quite a deep cellar, which was full of water because the river flooded, and whoever had been in the house before us had chopped half the steps away. You couldn't see that it had half the steps chopped away because the water was so high, but after four steps, there were no more, just a huge drop!'

There was indeed a particularly bad spate of flooding in the town in 1946, and the Blakewater, which flows close to the south side of King Street, burst its banks. Houses in the Whalley Banks area, close to where Jo lived, could only be reached by boat.

She remembers it was bad, but not unusual: 'Almost all of the houses that we lived in had cellars, and they were often flooded, though not Derwent Street. King Street had a cellar, the next house in Whalley Bank had a cellar, and then the next, Henry Street, had a huge cellar. We kept the coal there of course, and if Blakewater broke its banks and flooded it, then one of my brothers would have to go swimming for the coal down there, bringing up pieces of coal while another brother would wait on the steps with a bucket until it was full!'

Fine cotton yarn is less likely to break in damp conditions, and a century earlier weavers' cottages were deliberately sited close to water and, later, given deep, damp cellars. This is why cellars played so prominent a part in Jo's early life, spent in old weavers' cottages. During a government inspection in 1840, Joseph Kennedy

Flooding in Church Street, where Charles Tiplady had his shop. 'When the Blakewater flooded over and flooded the cellar,' recalls Jo, 'when my brothers went down to fetch the coal, one would go swimming down there, the other would wait on the steps with the bucket. And you'd keep bringing up pieces of coal to fill the bucket.'

reported finding men and women spinning and weaving in 'cold, dark, damp cellars without any fire or means of ventilation... the atmosphere on entering was literally foetid with the breath of the inmates.'

One hundred years later, one of these cellars was worrying a little girl so bad that it was enough to keep her out of the house as often as possible. 'The Henry Street cellar was the one that went into the early stories, a great big cellar, it was quite scary, that one. I remember seeing rats running around our feet in the toilet and water running into the cellar.' In Jo's imagination the cellar is a place of terror. For example, for little Kelly in *Somewhere, Someday*, it is a safe place from her abusive father.

My mam told my brother Michael that when it got really bad, he was to take me down to the coal cellar – you couldn't hear anything down there. We'd huddle together in the dark and he'd tell me stories of little people with wings and pointed feet, and how they lived in the cellar and hid whenever we went down.' She smiled. 'He said that if you believed in them, they would grant a wish. I believed it all, and wished to go away and never come back.' The quiet smile

Old weavers' cottages in Henry Street, photographed in 1953, when Jo still lived in the street. These differed from the majority of mill cottages in that the handloom shop was in the cellar. One hundred years earlier, Joseph Kennedy reported finding men and women spinning and weaving in 'cold, dark, damp cellars without any fire or means of ventilation... the atmosphere literally foetid with the breath of the inmates.'

melted beneath the sadness. 'But the beating went on, and I stopped believing.'

After King Street, the family moved to Whalley Bank, which, like the other houses, was owned by the council. 'Whalley Bank came up while we were waiting for Henry Street to become available,' Jo explained. It was a very fleeting visit and I don't remember a lot about that. Henry Street came into play when I was eight, nine. Henry Street was a happy house. I mean, we were poor and everything, we were short of food and clothes and all that, but we we had lots of laughs in that house.

Henry Street, like Derwent Street, is no more, but as the map on page 55 shows, it was slap bang in the centre of things, close to the market square.

Regent Street, where Marcia Bendall lived in *Angels Cry Sometimes*, ran across the top of Henry Street, and she gives us clear directions from the railway station by the Boulevard:

The walk from the Tram Boulevard to Regent Street, where Marcia and her family lived, took no more than five minutes – along by the shops, down Penny

Blackburn Railway Station leading on to Tram Boulevard (right) in the 1950s.

'There was hustle and bustle all around; porters rushing to and fro; passengers coming and going; train whistles shrieking; and in the huge arches that fronted the station a small girl and a woman were approaching every likely customer who might buy their flowers...' Don't Cry Alone

Street, then in past the Ship pub and over the Brown Street bridge to the little cobbled back street which had been home for Marcia for almost six years now.

Marcia had no liking for this particular journey; especially late in the year, like now. The back streets here were badly lit, with the lamps flickering ominously low, and sending out eerie shadows which made a body feel uncomfortably threatened. During the day, when God's natural light illuminated the darker corners, there was little to fear; but under the disguise of darkness, a body could be forgiven for imagining that all manner of creatures might suddenly emerge.

Marcia shivered. And she fancied it wasn't just from the cold. Night was thickening and all about her dark looming shadows moved in at alarming speed. Drawing her coat tightly about her, she hurried along – the tip-tap of her clogs on the flagstones echoing loudly into the silence, making her even more nervous.

As she neared the bridge just before Henry Street, Marcia was suddenly aware of other hurrying figures some way ahead.

Sixty years earlier, in 1868 in *Don't Cry Alone*, Beth Ward arrives at Blackburn Station, and the first people she comes across are Maisie and Cissie Armstrong, market flower sellers selling their wares:

It was near midday when Beth stepped out of the railway carriage at Blackburn Station, weary from her long journey and so hungry that her stomach was playing a tune inside her. She went steadily across the station... There was hustle and bustle all around; porters rushing to and fro; passengers coming and going;

The Boulevard, teeming with life in the 1950s, leads from the station on to Railway Road, then across Salford Bridge into the market area, at the top of which was Henry Street, where Jo lived. *See map, page 55.*

'It seemed to Phoebe that all life congregated here. People in a hurry poured out of the railway station. There were smart and upright businessmen in black suits and trilbys; other men, stooped and weary, making their way back from various factories, flat caps pulled down and heavy-booted feet trudging their way home. There were groups of giggling young women, and families clustered together as they wended in and out of the moving trams. And all around the noise rose up like the hum of a million bees in flight.'

Jessica's Girl

train whistles shrieking; and in the huge arches that fronted the station a small girl and a woman were approaching every likely customer who might buy their flowers...

Outside the station, Beth glanced down at the address which the Station Master had given her, and then folded the paper into her pocket. Pausing a moment to gather her strength, she looked out across the open square: at the carts rumbling along; at the people going about their business; at the ruddy-faced men in their short jackets and flat caps or sober coats and toppers; at the women in their dark fringed shawls, children running beside them; other women, grander, dressed in broad-brimmed feathered hats and gowns that swept the cobbles...

Raising her face to the sky... she wondered nervously what this town of Blackburn might have in store for her.

Later we learn from the little urchin, Cissie, how she gets to the port at Liverpool to buy the flowers for market – 'First thing this morning, I cadged a ride on a barge that were going to Liverpool docks... I was sure there'd be some flowers coming in from one o' them far-off countries. But there weren't! At least I never clapped eyes on 'em, that's for sure. Then I hid in a waggon coming back, and it went all the way round Lancashire afore ending up in Blackburn.'

It is not surprising that there is a central place for the market in Jo's imaginative vision of Blackburn. Long before the cotton industry took hold, the market had been the fulcrum of life in the town, and from the 1940s it was Jo's own playground. It opened on

The Brown Street bridge mentioned in Marcia's walk from Tram Boulevard to Regent Street (page 52) was the iron bridge over the Blakewater shown here in the middle distance. The river is low, the houses on the left are in Henry Street. The view is taken in 1958 from Union Street Bridge up the Blakewater towards Regent Street. See 1939 map for route, river, Cicely Bridge Mill, station, etc.

this particular site on January 28, 1848, prompting a local printer and bookseller, Charles Tiplady, to write verses to this 'day of honour to the Town...' Twice a week – on Wednesdays and Saturdays – the 350-stall bazaar set a challenge on a national scale. It also hosted an annual Easter Fair, and a year-round series of speakers, preachers and entertainers.

In *Alley Urchin*, Emma Grady's daughter, Molly, is taken for a thief in the market. In *Tomorrow The World*, Joe Tidy has a draper's stall there, and in *Cradle of Thorns*, cheeky, one-eared, Irish, rag-and-boneman Joe has a weekend stall, where he 'sold everything from old boots to copper boilers'. In *Whistledown Woman*,

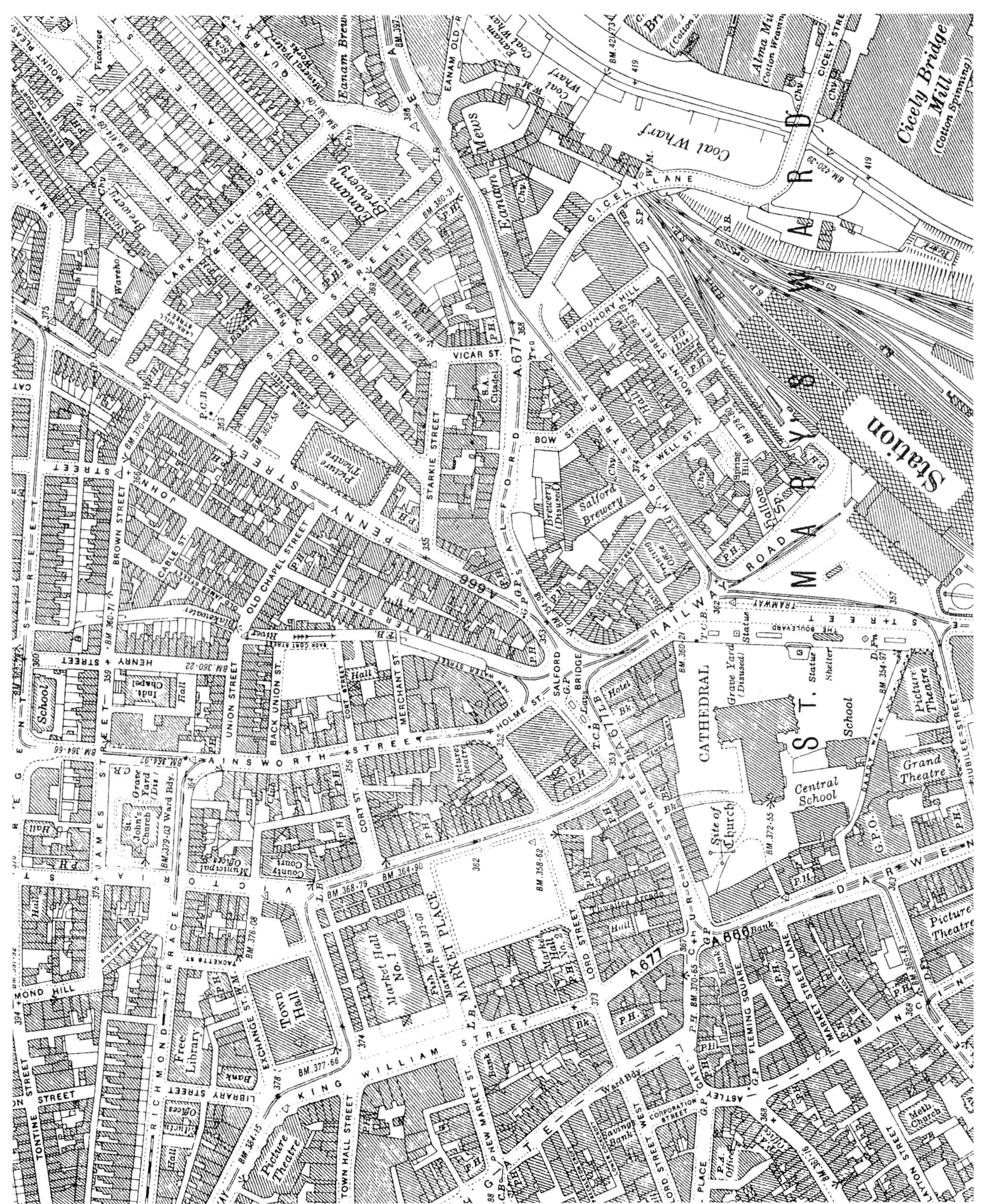

Rona Leum, the gypsy, works there while living out at Shillington in the district of Church, and in *Take This Woman*, set in the late 1940s, Sonny Fareham is fascinated by it – vendors shouting their wares, winking and joking as she walked by. Stray dogs dodging around her ankles to snatch up any juicy titbit that fell to the ground, and irate children bawling and screaming while their mothers raised eyes to heaven and wondered why they ever came out that morning. But Jo's personal vision is surely that of Queenie in *Her Father's Sins*:

And oh, what a treat it was when she and Auntie Biddy took the walk into town on a market day! Happen they'd be carrying a pair of Aunty Biddy's boots which needed the holes mending. Old Dubber Butterfield would sit on his three-legged stool amidst the hundreds of boots, shoes and clogs which hung from walls and ceilings, then with the great iron hobbling-foot between his knees and with a practised flick of his wrist he'd fit the boots onto it, shape a fresh-smelling piece of leather over the holes and, taking the little nails one at a time form between his teeth, he'd tap-tap and shape until the worn holey leather on Aunty Biddy's boots became a brand new sole.

Just occasionally, the two of them would go into Nan Draper's where every wall was piled high with shelves upon shelves of different sorts of cloth. Brown tweed; herringbone; flannel; winceyette, worsted . . . oh, there was no

19th-century Blackburn Market, as Molly Tanner and Beth Ward knew it.

'She looked out across the open square: at the carts rumbling along, at the people going about their business, at the ruddy-faced men in their short jackets and their flat caps or sober coats and toppers, at the women in their dark fringed shawls, children running beside them...' Don't Cry Alone

In Alley Urchin, *Molly, is taken for a thief in the market. '"Stop thief!" The shrill cry of alarm rang through Blackburn market-place and, instantly, all eyes were turned in one direction... "See!" cried the woman, waving her handkerchief in the direction of a small, dark-haired waif who was making good her escape. "There she is! Stop her, somebody . . ."'*

As early as the 16th century, Blackburn was a flourishing market town. When the market opened on the King William Street site shown here, on January 28, 1848, the 72-foot Italian-style clock tower became a focal point. On top of it was erected an 18-foot pole, up which a copper ball, 4 feet in diameter and 15 stones in weight, would rise at noon, dropping an hour later to signal the one o'clock gun, fired four days a week up to 1931.

This picture must have been taken at some time between 1903 and 1924, a period when the ball was out of action.

end to it. And here, Auntie Biddy would purchase her darning wool and thimbles, together with various sized needles. Queenie could remember the purchase of a measure of heavy brown cotton-material only once. Auntie Biddy explained that this rare luxury was necessary in the name of decency, as she was obliged to keep the two of them from 'falling into rags'. As far as Queenie was concerned, she was right glad Auntie Biddy had prevented such a thing. The idea of 'falling into rags' sounded a frightening prospect.

A dilly-dallying walk round the market, though, was something of a magic time for Queenie. Now and then they would stop at the liquorice stall and buy a threepenny bag of liquorice sticks and coltsfoot rock; then perhaps another time they might linger at Jud's corner stall, where amidst the colour and the shouting, the smells of roasting chestnuts and baking tatties, they would enjoy a glass of Jud's black frothy sarsaparilla. It all fascinated Queenie. And she had come to love Blackburn as fervently as did her Auntie Biddy...

Queenie loved it all. She derived the greatest satisfaction and enjoyment from watching and listening to all the familiar sounds which carried her above the mundane loneliness and boredom of her own existence. Queenie had

In The Devil you Know, *set in the 1950s, Sonny Fareham is fascinated by the market when she arrives in Blackburn for the first time: 'All around her vendors shouted their wares, winking and joking as she walked by. Stray dogs dodged around her ankles to snatch up any juicy titbit that fell to the ground, and irate children bawled and screamed while their mothers raised eyes to heaven and wondered why they ever came out that morning. "Little sods!" one poor soul yelled as her three offspring drove her to distraction. "Just wait till I tell your father what a time you've given me. Your arse will be ringing a tune, I can promise you that!"'*

For Jo's family in the same period, the market was a particular godsend. 'My mother had an awful job finding the money to feed us, and Sunday was the only good meal we had. She had a big enamel bowl, we would go on the market and collect all the bruised fruit and vegetables, and she would cook the vegetables with lumps of meat she got from the butcher in this big bowl and then put it on the table.'

always seen Blackburn market as a magic carpet and when a body climbed aboard it would be transported to another world . . . a fairytale world where round every corner a new adventure waited. So many times Auntie Biddy had brought her here, and even now, after all this time, the magic was not lost to Queenie. Tossed into the hub of activity and camouflaged beneath the great umbrellas of red and white awnings which covered every stall down every avenue, touching each other until the sky itself was obliterated by this spreading, billowing roof, Queenie took delight in all about her and the cautious step of her feet against the jutting cobbles became a carefree skip.

Jo describes the layout of the interior of the house she lived in in

'We were poor, we were short of food and clothes and all that, but we had lots of laughs in that house in Henry Street...'

Henry Street as Marcia Bendalls' Regent Street house in *Angels Cry Sometimes*: 'There were rumours that the Council had drawn up plans to acquire many such dwellings as the Bendalls', to install lavatories and such like,' Jo writes in the novel, 'but up to now, these well-intentioned plans had been confined only to the drawing-board. So Marcia and her family continued to make the best of what they'd got.' As, indeed, did Mary Jane and her family

'Although there was a lot of laughter and we made our own fun, the hardship was always there and we often went hungry,' Jo recalls. 'My mother had an awful job finding the money to feed us, and Sunday was the only good meal we had. She had a big enamel bowl, we would go on the market and collect all the bruised fruit and vegetables, and she would cook the vegetables with lumps of meat she got from the butcher in this big bowl and then put it on the table, in the centre, and we would all sit round. And – I am going to get lynched for saying this – the priest would arrive and eat half our dinner! I hated it. I said, "You shouldn't let him come in!" and my mam'd say, "Oh, you've got to let the priest come in." I think they were a little bit afraid of the priest. He was a Roman Catholic priest of course. They didn't take religion... they were not sort of fanatical religious people. The priest would always come along, and I remember he would say to her, "You haven't been to church, have you Mary?"

'"I'll be along," she'd say.

'But she never would go along.

'If there wasn't much money coming in at the end of the week, we'd go hungry. But I thought that was how life was. Only when I went to school did I realise we were really poor, that I was different from other people living in better streets. We had a lot of well-to-do kids coming to the school [St Anne's on Feilden and Prince's Street] from better areas, who were quite nicely dressed, would wear the uniform. I was going to the new school and had to have a uniform. Well me mam couldn't afford a uniform. So she took me down to the rag-and-bone shop. I had to have a blue mac with the belt and hood. Now if you had a penny you had to rummage on the ground to see what you could find, but if you had threepence you could go on the rack – things hanging on coat hangers! Posh things. And me mam found me a Gaberdine mac. So I wore it very proudly to school on Monday morning, and we were all lining up to go into the classrooms, and these girls behind me were sniggering and laughing. And I thought, they're laughing at me! Why are they laughing at me? And I knew why they were laughing when I got into the cloakroom because there was a name tag sticking out of my coat, and it was one of theirs! So their mam had given it to the rag-and-bone man. They knew where I had got it from. So I threw it away on the way home and got a hiding from me mam!

Jo's readers may remember the enamel bowl for the Sunday

'Only when I went to school did I realise we were really poor... We had a lot of well-to-do kids coming to the school [St Anne's] from better areas, who were quite nicely dressed, would wear the uniform. I was going to the new school and had to have a uniform. Well me mam couldn't afford a uniform. So she took me down to the rag-and-bone shop...

hot pot making an appearance on the table of Lizzie and Ted Miller's house in *Nobody's Darling*. Here, their daughter, Ruby, explains to her posh friend, Maureen, what it really means to be hungry-poor:

Being poor frightens me more than anything in the world. Money could buy so much happiness. I know that now. All the time our dad's been out of work, our mam's been hard put to feed the family. I've seen her push her own food on to

...and these girls behind me were sniggering and laughing. And I thought, they're laughing at me! Why are they laughing at me? And I knew why they were laughing when I got into the cloakroom because there was a name tag sticking out... and it was one of theirs! Their mam had given it to the rag-and-bone man. They knew where I had got it from!'

the young 'uns' plates when she thought no one was looking, and at night when she's sent us all to bed while she waits downstairs for our dad, I've heard her crying. For years, she's worn the same two skirts and the same tattered old shawl. There's never enough food in the cupboard, and we don't have enough blankets to keep us warm, even on a summer's night. In the winter we have to count the number of cobs we put on the fire, and even when our dad was in work, there were times when he had to walk because he couldn't afford the tramfare. Our mam always puts on a brave face, but I know how she's feeling inside, and I can't stand it.

Jo's novel *Cradle of Thorns* is all about the noble values engendered by poverty and the idea that we are, all of us, born into our own

'There was poverty with the men earning a pittance from the cotton mills and factories hereabouts, and the women raising hordes of children; ragged snotty-nosed children, who filled the street with their laughter and sat on the kerbstones with their feet dangling in the gutter.'

A Little Badness

cradle of suffering. How we deal with our particular 'thorny problem' is all; being born out of wedlock is the heroine Nell Reece's thorny problem. It is a powerful title, and I asked Jo where it came from.

'When I was thinking about that particular book, several titles came to me. I was looking for the *feeling* of how it was for us at home,' she replied. 'Now, my younger brother, when he was born, I was about five, and I remember vividly my mother bringing him

Looking up Birley Street to Larkhill beyond.

home from hospital and his cradle was an orange box lined with newspaper in front of the fire. That came to me while I was thinking about that book. All of us, all of us children, never had a warm cradle, a pretty cradle... I chose that wood, the thorns, I think, because it is evocative of suffering... you are not *supposed* to suffer when you are a child, you are not *supposed* to be uncomfortable, you are supposed to be cossetted and warm and safe. But at home there was never food in the cupboards. We lived each day as it came and life was very difficult.

'I am talking about the kind of poverty that you really can't get to grips with unless you have been through it. During my childhood, we never had any cups in our house, only jam-jars or milk bottles to drink out of. As soon as I could afford it, I started buying dinner services. At the last count I had ten! But now, when I can have whatever I want materially, I haven't changed inside... because you cannot forget. You cannot lose it, even though I know that I'll never have to go to the rag-and-bone man again.

'My mother always knew when the rent man would turn up and sometimes we would hide down behind the settee and she would dare us to breathe a word. He would go away, but you always knew he'd be back. Sometimes he would try and catch you out. He'd wait round the corner and see if you came out.'

Property men get a lashing in the novels. John Harvey is the unscrupulous property agent in *Somewhere, Someday* – 'a nasty, sly sort...mid-forties, fancies himself with the ladies...a tight-fisted bastard an' all.' Kelly Wilson gets the better of him and reclaims the sometime family home, but rent man David Miller in *Don't Cry Alone* is a quite different sort, on the face of it mild-mannered and compassionate, but soon we discover that he is a hopelessly weak man, blindly loyal to his boss, Luther Reynolds, who lives in smart Buncer Lane and who is the worst kind of mean, miserly agent, as Cockney Tyler Blacklock discovers from a Blackburn auctioneer:

Right old Scrooge he is an' all. Thinks nothing of screwing the last farthings outta ordinary hard-working folk whose misfortune it is to reside in one of his run-down properties. But, you see, ordinary folk don't get much choice in where they live. My own mother still inhabits a disgusting damp hovel down Larkhill.

He eyed Tyler with curiosity, recalling the distinct London accent. 'Being as you're not from these parts, you wouldn't be acquainted with the facts regarding Larkhill, now would you sir? Larkhill being a street of back-to-backs, and one of that old fellow's most infamous holdings.' He paused only to draw breath before going on, 'Burned down it did . . . almost the entire stretch of Larkhill on one side. Burned to the ground by a fire started in Maisie Armstrong's place . . . had a lodger she did. The word was given out was that the young widder were a relative. Anyway, the fire took Maisie and two other good souls beside.'

...Since the fire that devastated Larkhill, that canny old villain has wriggled out of every opportunity to put the street to rights. My own mother lives in fear of her very life, what with fire-ravaged timbers hanging loose in mid-air, and rats running free round the rubble. It's nothing short of a nightmare for them that's left in Larkhill, and that old scoundrel still demands four shillings a week rent. Can you imagine that, eh? Four shillings a week, and most poor working folk have only twenty shilling a week between themselves and the workhouse! But do you think anybody gives a cuss. No, they don't!'

Richard Jackson's corner shop on Johnston Street.

'It was all swings and roundabouts. The corner shop let my mam buy things against money coming in on Friday, and if the money didn't come in on Friday she'd pawn my dad's best trousers to pay the shop bill.'

In *Don't Cry Alone*, little Cissie Armstrong, the market flower seller, lives with her mother, Maisie, in one of 'the long stretch of houses on Larkhill', up behind Henry Street – Luther Reynolds' patch. Maisie gets seriously behind with the rent, and then she is consumed in a horrific fire, telling Beth Ward in her dying breath to look after 'the childer'. This dreadful scene was once again inspired by personal experience.

'When I was about ten I had a friend who lived two streets away from me,' Jo said. 'I loved her very much. She was my very best friend of all; you know, as a kid you do have a very best friend. Her mother had just had a baby, and she was very excited about this. We came home from school that Friday and we were running because we wanted to see the baby. So we saw the baby, and then I went home and played in the street and did whatever I normally did. My friend was going to look after her mam that weekend, as she had just come out of hospital, so she had said to me that she wouldn't be coming out to play, she would see me on Monday morning. I said I would come and call for her to walk to school, which is what I did every day.

'I spent most of that weekend over at my Grandma Harrison's in Accrington, coming back late Sunday night on the tram and going straight to bed. Monday morning I went to call for Rita and knocked on the door and her dad came out and he was just sobbing uncontrollably. I said, "I have come for Rita," and he looked at me and said, "She's dead."

'I was young and didn't know what to do – you know, you are riveted to the ground, you don't know what he is talking about.. What do you *mean*, she's dead? And I just ran home, started screaming and ran home, and my mam sat me down and told me. "I was hoping you wouldn't find out," she said, but she should have known better. She must have known that I would find out. She told me that Rita had been looking after her mother and the bed had been moved into the front room, and Rita had got a little pinny on. Rita was waiting on her mum and helping with the baby and there was a big fire on because it was winter. It caught Rita's pinny and nobody could put the flames out... My best friend was burned to death. That has never left me. So, the fire, I think, springs from that time. '

Unlike Maisie Armstrong, Jo's mum was never in serious debt. 'She was working in between having all the children, so she brought money in, but there was always this *fear* of debt, that you could be carted off... She was always frightened of that.

'It was all swings and roundabouts. The corner shop let my mam buy things against

The Swan and the Sun are next to one another in King Street. 'Quickly, before she might look out of the window and see him, he hurried along King Street, up to the top, and across to the Swan Inn. Here he knew he would find a friend or two to help him drown his sorrows.' Tom Mulligan in Tomorrow The World

'A busy old inn, set on the corner of King Street... there'd been more punch-ups and differences of opinion in that place than anywhere else in the whole of Blackburn. But it was a long-time, favourite meeting place.' Cradle of Thorns

money coming in on Friday, and if the money didn't come in on Friday she'd pawn my dad's best trousers to pay the shop bill.

'Everyone in our street was poor. Like the rest, my father worked extremely long hours. They had to because they had all these children. I mean, many of the families down the street had lots of children. So the mothers were busy having the children and the men had to work to provide, and come the Friday, they were worn out, they headed for the pub with the wages. It was a vicious circle.

'Before the Navigation, the Sun was my dad's Friday night haunt. It was not far from Henry Street. On a Friday night my mam would wait, and it would be six o'clock in the evening and then it would be eight o'clock and she'd say, "Tha' dad's not home lass. He's down the pub, go 'n' fetch him. "I was only about seven, I suppose. You wouldn't do that now, because you'd be terrified your kid would be snatched, but I'd go down the pub and knock on the door and a big navvy would come out, "Aw, it's Barney's lass," he'd say, "fetch her in." And he'd bring me in and stand me on the counter and I'd sing and dance, and me dad would put his flat cap next to me and they'd all put money into it. I wouldn't let him have the money, though. "That's me mam's money, not yours dad!" I'd say.'

Two families in need, more than half a century apart. Recalling for me how she used to dance on the bar of the Sun gave Jo 'a warm glow,' but she is aware of the compounding effect drink has on poverty, of the repercussions within her family as within the families of many of her friends in her neighbourhood.

The Sun at the top corner of King Street is still there and features strongly in Jo's books, as indeed does the Swan next door. Old Sal discusses both in *Alley Urchin*, for example, and in *Looking Back*, Jack Mason, Amy Tattersall's former lover with whom she runs away, tells her that 'Most nights I'm to be found in the Sun public house, top of King Street.' In *Cradle of Thorns*, Molly Davidson dares to go in and order 'two pints of yer best,' and she is ordered out. In 1890, when this novel is set, respectable women were not welcome in pubs. The Sun was frequented mainly by men...

...men of all ages and means. There had been more punch-ups and differences of opinion in that place than anywhere else in the whole of Blackburn. But it was a long-time, favourite meeting place. On Saturday it was a haven for all those men who sought refuge from the many trials of a working life. They might be seeking relief from a long, demanding week in the pits some distance from their homes, or the mills on their doorsteps, or their wives and families, or they'd be sneaking a quiet drink away from their clinging sweethearts. Whatever the reason, they flocked there by the dozen, propping up the bar and staggering home when the last shout was called.

By the time of *Looking Back*, a novel set in 1948, young Sandra Craig is not only brazen enough to believe that she has a right to drink in a pub, she openly exercises and abuses that right. However, in *Her Father's Sins*, set around the same time, Jo can still write, 'No respectable lass would ever be seen in a pub; unless rightly invited. And even then, they would know their place. So the women often preferred to stay at home and darn their men's socks, bathe their countless offspring and count the dwindling brass which they skilfully hid from the "old man" with his appetite for boozing.' Today, Jo confirms that it was a transition time in all sorts of ways for women: 'A lot of the women were rebelling at the straitjacket that they'd be placed in, particularly in the 1950s. They were going out and they were forcing their way into the pubs. If the men can go in, I can go in, you know?'

So, what did Mary Jane do when money was short? I thought of Queenie, whose pride prevented her 'going begging' to welfare. In the Kenney family's case, 'poverty, real degrading poverty, had crept up on them,' and was symbolised by the Cob o' Coal. 'Nine feet tall with a skirt dimension of twenty feet or more, it was raw and shiny black, hard as the day it was wrestled out by the miners from its long resting place beneath the ground.' It had been given a shiny brass plaque and transported to its place at the corner of Pump Street and Waterfall Mill to the accompaniment of the town band. Raw rock-coal, unsuitable for burning, but the need of the poor folk was such that within six years it had been reduced to 'a hump-backed deformity of which no-one could be proud, least of all the coal-merchants', who had brought it.

For Jo's mum, 'the answer was the convent, Nazareth House,' Jo recalls. 'The old house, the Victorian house, has gone, but the convent is still where it always was, off Preston New Road. The first time I heard about Nazareth House, I suppose I was about eight and my mother said one day, "Get your coat on lass," and she told Winnie to get her coat on and she put the two babbies in the pram, and we walked and it seemed like never ending. I was actually crying I was so tired, and we walked right through Blackburn, right along the Preston New Road, and it must have been five or six miles, I suppose.

'When we got there, she pushed us up this path of beautiful rhododendrons to the house at the top, the big convent, sat us on the benches out front with the tramps and told us, "Sit there." And so we would, and she would knock on the door and the Mother Superior and one of the sisters would come out and say, "It's all right, sit there," and she'd give my mam half a crown and we could run out on the lawn. It was lovely, we'd never seen a lawn! You could actually play on grass! Then she'd come out with a tray of big chipped enamel mugs of tea and great big thick butties plastered with dripping. They'd feed us and give me mam a few bob.'

Here, in *Her Father's Sins*, Queenie arrives at the convent for the first time:

The gates of Nazareth House. 'When we got there, she pushed us up this path of beautiful rhododendrons to the house at the top and sat us on the benches out front with the tramps... The sisters would feed us and give me mam a few bob.'

'The winding bends up the bank to the convent...' and, shown here, the convent grotto.

Poverty brings us to the role of religion in Jo's life, to Father Riley, to the Blackburn Ragged School, to the Salvation Army and to the Convent of Nazareth House. 'This convent plays a very large part in my memory. Coming up through those gates just now... Mum used to walk us, it must be five miles from where we used to live, to here. We knew we were coming to have a meal, so we'd nearly run all the way because it was a treat.'

Almost at once they rounded a crook in the lane, and directly before them was a wide open gateway bearing a board which read:

The Convent of Nazareth House

To the left of the broad gravelled driveway, a narrow footpath followed the winding bends up the bank to the convent. Queenie trailed behind Auntie Biddy, her excited chatter temporarily silenced by the awesome solitude and magnificent sights all around her. The whispering willows touched and teased them as they passed by, and the bright songs of birds filled the air with happiness. Queenie felt as though this day she'd been whisked off to paradise.

On reaching the top of the winding footpath, Queenie and Auntie Biddy found themselves entering a kind of open courtyard, surrounded by sweeping lawns and colourful shrubberies.

'Oh, Auntie Biddy!' Queenie could hardly believe her eyes. 'It's beautiful!'

'Aye lass,' Auntie Biddy was slow in recovering from the steep climb and her words were strangled, 'it is that. But I still wonder how folks living in such luxury can ever understand folks like us. It don't sit right in my mind!'

Nazareth House stood proudly before them: a great sprawling mansion of grotesque proportions. Its Victorian origin was evident in the additions of

'All the ragged kids went to the Blackburn Ragged School. We had to go into the Assembly Hall and pray. We all had to stand there with our heads bowed and pray. Then we'd get fed. Then, if we were lucky we would go on a charabanc to Blackpool.

ugly haphazard extensions, jutting out at most peculiar angles from both wings of the house. At either side of the central oaken door, wooden-slatted benches rested beneath towering golden conifers.

Queenie's eyes were drawn to the eccentric-looking figure seated on the right-hand bench. The tramp looked up to meet her gaze. 'Morning, young missie,' he said. He was dressed in a long, heavy black coat which reached right down to the floor, all but covering his thick mud-spattered boots. Around his waist, from the frayed string which secured his buttonless coat, hung various artefacts including a white enamel mug covered in dark chipped patches, and a collection of eating tools tied round the ends by a thinner piece of string.

A few years ago, a television company did a short documentary film of Jo's life in Blackburn, and naturally wanted to include a trip to Nazareth House. 'They had to drag me up there, it was very emotional for me. This convent plays a very large part in my memory. Going up through those gates and coming up through the lane... it was so nostalgic. Mam had to be a bit desperate before she would go up there. The nuns used to come out and talk to you, with their black gowns and white cowl on the forehead... .they were very formidable and quite daunting, but they were kind and they would talk. They seemed very surreal to me at first.

'I put Nazareth House into Cherry Tree [a smart area to the south west of the town centre] when I wrote *Her Father's Sins*, though the convent is actually along the Preston New Road. I rang up the Mother Superior to see if I could use the convent for many of the scenes concerning my mother and she was delighted, but, "Don't say where we are!" So I then got all these letters telling me that I had put Nazareth House in the wrong place!'

This is a Blackburn Ragged School outing as the 19th century gave way to the 20th, their Sunday best, possibly better than would have been mustered half a century later: 'Christmas time they had two queues going down to these big tea boxes, filled with toys that the well-off kids had brought in,' recalls Jo. ' The girls would queue one side and the boys the other, because of course there'd be girl toys and boy toys. I remember this particular Christmas I had this one-legged teddy, and I had that teddy for years afterwards. I loved it to bits. I mean we were lucky if we got an apple for Christmas, at home, you know?'

Another local sanctuary for the poor was the Blackburn Ragged School, in Bent Street, close to Derwent Street and still there today. Ragged schools were originally free elementary schools for poor children. In 1843, Charles Dickens went to visit one in Little Saffron Hill, London, the very street where Fagin had his notorious den. He wrote that 'the name [Ragged Schools] implies the purpose. They who are too ragged, wretched, filthy and forlorn, to enter any other place: who could gain admission into no charity-school, and who would be driven from any church door: are invited to come in here, and find some people not depraved, willing to teach them something, and show them some sympathy, and stretch a hand out, which is not the hand of Law, for their correction...'

When Jo attended the Blackburn Ragged School, there appears to have been no academic curriculum of any kind, indeed that was not its point. It was more of a Church-sponsored charity: 'If you went there and sang hymns on a Sunday, then you'd get fed. We went there often. From the age of four until I was about nine.'

This is interesting because the academic education of mill workers was not a priority of mill owners in 19th-century Blackburn, either, while they did believe that their *moral* education had clear advantages. As a consequence, they were a major sponsor of Sunday Schools: 'Those workmen and work women who are most sober, steady, respectable and intelligent have been or still are, connected with Sunday schools,' wrote mill owner John Baynes, who had Cicely Bridge Mill and spoke for many with an eye to profitably smooth management/worker relations. Another driving force behind these schools was a determination on the part of the mill master that his workers' families would attend a school sponsored by the Church to which he was affiliated. It was all part of the clubby culture with which he controlled his workers.

I asked Jo whether there was a very strict regime at the Ragged School. 'We were never allowed to address any of the women there by their first names,' she remembers. 'There was a woman there, was she called Mrs Parker? And I gave her this name, Sarah, in *Her Father's Sins*. She was very kind. They were all very kind. All volunteers. Christian people.'

'Why did you go there?' I asked

'All the ragged kids went there,' she replied.

'Why? To have a good time?'

'You must be joking! We had to go into the Assembly Hall and pray. We all had to stand there with our heads bowed and pray. Then we'd get fed. Then, if we were lucky, we would go in a charabanc to Blackpool, and at Christmas time they'd have two queues going down to these big tea boxes, filled with toys that the well-off kids had brought in. The girls would queue one side and the boys the other, because of course there'd be girl toys and boy toys. I remember one particular Christmas, I picked this one-legged teddy, and I had that teddy for years afterwards. I loved it to bits. I mean we were lucky if we got an apple for Christmas, at home, you know?'

I thought of Queenie getting 'a spherical object carefully wrapped up by Auntie Biddy' as a birthday treat, and how grateful she had been 'It was an orange, a big Jaffa with thick pocked skin which shot out gas and juice as Queenie greedily tore it away from the segments. She had delighted in sucking into those fat segments when the bitter sweet juices flowed into her mouth, making her nose sting and twisting her features into such protesting grimaces that might have frightened the devil himself! Queenie had thoroughly enjoyed her birthday treat and she was quick to tell Auntie Biddy so...'

'Did you not feel that going to the Ragged School was marking you out as different?' I asked.

'I never felt victimised by life, because I love life,' Jo replied.

Queenie turned the words over and over in her mind. 'Blackburn Ragged School'. They had a sad ring about them, and their implications frightened her. She refused to dwell on the matter, thankful that her hand stayed well and truly fast inside the security of Auntie Biddy's.

She looked up now at the mention of her name. 'Queenie! Pay attention, lass.' Auntie Biddy shook her gently by the hand. 'Father Riley's after telling you about your birthday surprise.'

Father Riley led Queenie and her Auntie Biddy over to the long wooden tables, where he gestured for them to take a seat on the accompanying bench. 'Now then, little Queenie, do you want a glass of sarsaparilla, or a nice cup of Sarah's tea?'

Sarah beamed at them from her place behind the serving-hatch. Queenie, momentarily fascinated by the odd face-twitching way Sarah had of hoisting her rimless glasses up the considerable length of her nose, said smiling, 'A glass of sarsaparilla please.'

Father Riley swept away to collect the refreshments. Queenie's observant eyes travelled the length and breadth of the Hall. She didn't think it a very impressive place at all, more like a big tram shelter, she decided. The woodblocked floor was dull and considerably worn, especially in the immediate vicinity of Sarah's serving-hatch. The high daunting walls were distempered the most nauseating shade of shiny purple, and the few narrow slitted windows way up towards the ceiling were so grubby that even the bright filtered rays of watery spring sunshine lost their natural exuberance on struggling through.

Queenie thought it too depressing for words. She began to wish they hadn't come...

'Here we are then, one extra large glass of

sarsaparilla,' Father Riley slid the drink across the table to Queenie, before handing Auntie Biddy a cup and saucer, 'and one of Sarah's specials... There's so much noise in here, Biddy! Perhaps we could talk better in Sarah's kitchen?'

Sarah's kitchen was bigger than the whole of Auntie Biddy's house. Great black iron pans of enormous dimensions littered the endless array of shelves and benches. Three huge cooking ranges, blackleaded and polished till you could see your face in them, stretched away down the centre of the room as far as the eye could see. The red quarry-tiled floor shone with loving care and elbow grease.

Queenie felt pleasantly secure in this kitchen, and it heightened the immediate liking she had taken to the homely Salvation Army officer, Sarah... By no stretch of the imagination could Sarah be described as pretty. Queenie tried so hard not to stare at the bulbous warts which festooned the plump smiling face but somehow her eyes were constantly drawn back to them.

'Not very pretty lass, are they?' When Sarah smiled, as she did now, her white even teeth shone like pearls, and her whole face lit up. From behind the spectacles, her fair eyes danced cheekily. 'Haven't always resembled a wart-hog,' she laughed, putting the squirming Queenie instantly at ease, 'one o' these days, I might see what can be done about 'em; but they're no bother! I'm not out to win any beauty contests.'

Queenie decided she liked Sarah almost as much as she liked Auntie Biddy.

Father Riley's quiet voice addressed itself to Queenie. 'Auntie Biddy thinks, and so do I, that it would be nice for you to have a few more friends of your own age.' Queenie knew what he meant. She had no friends really, except for Sheila, and that had long been a source of concern to Auntie Biddy although it had never bothered Queenie... 'Every Easter,' he went on, 'the Ragged School children have a special surprise treat. It isn't very often that we can afford to go to the seaside; but this year,' he smiled knowingly at Sarah, 'thanks to help from our Salvation Army friends, we're all off to Blackpool – only for the day mind. Now then, Queenie, how would you like to come?'

Blackpool? The seaside! Queenie had always longed to go to the seaside, but she'd kept the dream simmering deep in her heart. She knew Auntie Biddy couldn't take her, so she'd accepted that it would have to remain a dream probably for a very long time to come. But now! 'The seaside? The real seaside, for a whole day?'

Father Riley took hold of Queenie's small hand. 'Yes, lass. The real seaside, with shells and crabs, and golden sand. It'll be grand, won't it?'

'Blackpool,' Jo remembers. 'We did actually go once – there were about thirty-six of us in this big charabanc, and we were all chattering and laughing and fighting on the floor, you know, all that. But when we got there, it was the first time I had ever seen the sea. I was absolutely floored by what I saw.

'This vast space of water meeting with the sky. It was just...just mind boggling. I stood on the sand for ages and ages just looking. It was huge, an awesome experience for me. The space and the brightness because you know at home the streets were very dark, the buildings, the cobbles. You'd have the lamps, and how I loved the street lamps, and the cobbles...but you had this closed-in feeling.

'First, when they said we were going to Blackpool, it meant little. I had heard of Blackpool, but when we got there I was just so amazed. God knows how long I stood there just staring at the space and this water and the brightness of everything. We only went once.'

Queenie doesn't in fact visit Blackpool with the Ragged School because Aunt Biddy's health is failing fast. She dies shortly afterwards from TB. Only in the later book, *Let Loose The Tigers*, does Queenie finally make it there. The year is 1965, both Queenie and her boyfriend, Rick, are there, and the trip turns into a disaster:

Queenie shifted about on the wooden-slatted seat and stretched her neck to peer out of the open-topped tram. It was bitingly cold up there on the top deck, with the wind sailing in from the sea and skimming the tram like a knife-edge. Her nose burning from the cold, the wispy fringes of hair driven back from her forehead and ears, she felt the wind like the sharp crack of a whip. But in all of her life Queenie could never remember experiencing such exhilaration. The tangy salt air flooded her nostrils and the rhythmic clatter of the tram's iron wheels against the metal sleepers reverberated through her like a second heartbeat.

Queenie's eyes were alive with excitement as

Right: *Blackpool beach, a beauty uncovered. 'This vast space of water meeting with the sky. It was just...just mind boggling.'*

'When we got there I was just so amazed. God knows how long I stood there just staring at the space...I stood on the sand for ages and ages just looking, because you know at home the streets were very dark, the buildings, the cobbles.'
Below: *'The tower of Blackpool rose up from the skyline like a giant twinkling ornament.'* Her Father's Sins

the tram shunted along. She greedily stored every sight: before her the tower of Blackpool rose up from the skyline like a giant twinkling ornament, providing a beacon for everything below.

Many of the shops would stay closed until Easter, when their windows and forecourts would display multitudes of colourful nonsense and little souvenirs for the merry holidaymakers to take home, for keeping alive the memory of a week or a day at Blackpool's seaside.

The gaily-painted gypsy wagons festooning the broad promenade, where the weather-skinned women held a client's trembling hand, to foretell a fortune of coming riches and maybe a tall, dark-skinned lover, were tightly shuttered against the unloving winter. Hanging overhead down the mile-long road hugging the promenade, Queenie's eager gaze feasted on glowing lamps and lighting paraphernalia of every shape, size, colour and description – of elves and gnomes, glass coaches and diamond stars. As Queenie gazed up at them, entranced as the small child who had once dreamed of coming to Blackpool, it was like a wonderland she would never ever forget...

Blackpool pier was considered to be one of the most popular in the country, and Rick could see why. It was an attractive old pier, built with great

'The child came out of nowhere, a flurry of red-chequered dress glimpsed out of the corner of his eye. Even as Rick stood up she was dipping beneath the balustrades… The pier had come alive with activity. The police ushered the people back and the coastguard launched immediate rescue.' Let Loose The Tigers

thick planks of wood, slatted together for walkways and leaving gaps between, showing the sea below. Right up the farthest reaches where the pier ended and the waters stretched out into an endless horizon, some of the boards had rotted and one or two of the handrails had warped and split because of the relentless salt winds.

This particular area was duly cordoned off against the public and detailed for a considerable sum of money to be spent in restoration; a conspicuously-placed board warned people away. Rick found a bench close by and there he sat to eat his sandwich, gazing towards where the sea lurched and slapped against the thick sturdy pier-legs; his mind conscious of little except that soon, quite soon he would find Queenie.

So steeped in thoughts of Queenie was he, that what happened next took him by complete surprise, triggering a reflex action which gave him no time for caution.

The child came out of nowhere, a flurry of red-chequered dress glimpsed out of the corner of his eye. Even as Rick stood up she was dipping beneath the balustrades and already running towards the rail at the end of the pier. Without delay, he was after her and running across the cordoned-off area,

with shouts of alarm from somewhere down the pier ringing in his ears. He could also hear his own voice, terrified for that child and urging her to stand still, to stop and stay exactly where she was... and though his heart trembled at the danger she was in, his voice came out to her in a calm controlled manner.

Now he could hear a woman screaming behind him, and when in a nerve-destroying sound of renting, splintering timber the child fell out of sight and into the swallowing waters, the woman's screams filled Rick's brain until he could see and hear little else.

It was only a matter of seconds before Rick had thrown off his coat and shoes and had launched himself into the air above the spot where he'd seen the child go down beneath the waters.

The pier had come alive with activity. The police ushered the people back and the coastguard launched immediate rescue. When they reached Rick, he held the live bundle up for them to take safely into the craft. And in that instant, the jagged timber made precarious by the child's fall wrenched itself loose to come crashing down about his head and shoulders. In his exhaustion Rick was unable to fend off the avalanche and, unconscious, he slithered from the sight of those who had watched in helpless horror. In his darkening mind he could see only Queenie and with her image came the sensation of it all being too late, for she was lost to him forever!

'Good Lord, Queenie lass!' cried Katy, her face drained of colour, 'Whatever's happened?' Queenie had no idea, but it was obvious that someone somewhere was in trouble... there was talk among the passengers of someone having been drowned. It was a man, they said, 'a young man who had given up his life to save a child'.

Let Loose The Tigers

It is incredible to think that just a few miles away from the dark mill colonies there could be such beauty – some of the best skies to be seen occur along this coast – yet they were out of reach of these children. Today, Jo's sister, Winifred, makes up for it: 'She is a story all to herself,' Jo tells me. 'Each year we say, "You can go anywhere you like in the world for a holiday," and she'll get all the brochures for the Seychelles and the Maldives and America, and my husband, Ken, says, "You know what she's going to say when she comes back." It happens every time. She says, "I want to go to Blackpool!" And off she goes and has a whale of a time.'

Escape

A strangely exhilarating sensation swept through her as she emerged from the relative darkness of the mill into the grey daylight behind the wide doors. She felt free! This would be the very first time since starting here that she hadn't spent a full weekday harnessed to the relentless demands of her spinning machine. As the gusty breeze blew against her face, Marcia greedily breathed it in. She'd been used to entering the mill in the dark and emerging at the end of the day, still in the dark. Daylight was something she only ever enjoyed on a weekend.

Marcia in *Angels Cry Sometimes*

Jo's trip to Blackpool was the only occasion she can recall leaving the streets of Blackburn as a child, farther than 'the wide-open fields and tree-lined avenues which belonged to that enviable outer part of Blackburn.' Whatever the joys of the Derwent Street and Henry Street communities, it is as well to remember just how dreary the streets were: 'The predominant impression which Blackburn leaves is that of grimness, unmitigated by any natural pleasantness,' read a report of *The Pilgrim Trust* in 1938, 'for the city is too large for

Blackburn in the 1950s, when there were 200 factory chimneys scraping the sky and the soot was said to blacken the fleece of sheep on the Pennine Hills up to 15 miles away.

'The tall mill chimneys belched out their fumes and the grey-black vapour settled like a dark cloud over the whole town, blotting out the sun and filling the air with specks of charcoal that irritated the throat and stung the eyes...'
Jessica's Girl

Below, *at 312 feet, the Audley Destructor, was the tallest.*

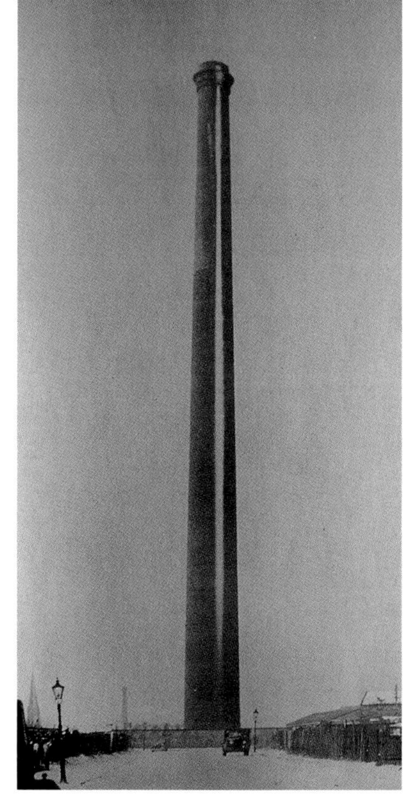

much sense of the surrounding country to penetrate it. Everywhere is a forest of tall black chimneys, against a sky that seems always drab, everywhere cobbled streets, with the unrelieved black of the mill girls' overalls and the clatter of wooden clogs.'

Forties' and fifties' Blackburn meant smoke and dirt, and smuts and grime coming out of the coal fires in the homes, fumes and chemicals from the industries. Jo herself talks of the 'closed-in feeling' of the maze of streets where she played, and of 'the houses dark and grim.' William Woodruff wrote in his autobiography, *The Road To Nab End*, that 'the air hung like lead' after he, as a boy, had returned to Blackburn following his first trip to Blackpool. On the way to school the boys and girls of Blackburn would see nothing but bricks and mortar and chimneys and streets, nothing but dreary fronts of houses and factories.

So, how is it that Jo can also write about the beauty of the townscape in *Nobody's Darling*? 'Brookhouse Mills made a daunting and magnificent sight. Like a monstrous stone cake, its grime-covered tiles were the chocolate icing and the long cylindrical chimneys were gigantic candles. The out-pouring smoke snaked through the sky, making weird dark patterns against the bright sunlight which in their very ugliness appeared uniquely beautiful.'

Again, in *Tomorrow The World*, which describes the Blackburn community of 1850, she writes, 'In this area of King Street, where houses lined the street and rows of chimneys pumped

Tram Boulevard, 1950s' smog. Yet, despite the pollution, it was all part of the magic of life at the time. 'At quarter to four the following morning, she was out of bed and watching from the window as the sky began to flood with light, silhouetting the irregular skyline with its array of chimneys, monumental cylindrical pipes rising from the cotton mills, together with the nearer squat chimneys jutting from the endless rows of back-to-back dwellings. Already the ascending curls of smoke were darkening the coming dawn...' Don't Cry Alone

dark, foul smoke into the air, there was little room for beauty. But the bridge was surprisingly pretty, gently curving over the canal, with fluted bricks and narrow pavements. Grime from the mill chimneys had darkened the stone, but it didn't matter. The bridge stood proud, and nothing, no smoke, or the ravages of time, or even the drunks who occasionally emptied the contents of their stomachs over it, could destroy its appeal for Bridget.'

Like Bridget Mulligan, Jo's vision of Blackburn is an imaginative vision, contoured by the emotions she experiences. To that extent Josephine Cox is creating Blackburn, just as Blackburn created her. She came to a town of soot and grime and dreary, closed-in streets, and left one of 'real flesh and blood people,' as she writes in her introduction. Jo's perception is influenced by the spirit of the community, by the character of life, but just as she needed to escape it in her youth, so she would need to be free of it for thirty years in order to make her adult vision coherent. For there were ghosts to lay.

As a child, grim poverty would have been enough to drive her to 'create a little world of my own to get into,' but beneath the surface there was another problem, about which Jo loathed to be reminded, but which threatened to find echoes in the grim reality of the streets outside.

Recalling for me how she used to sing and dance on the bar of the Sun gave her 'a warm glow,' but Jo, above all, is aware of the compounding effect drink has on poverty, of the repercussions within her family as within the families of many of her friends in her neighbourhood. That is the reason why, in *Cradle of Thorns*, Molly takes it upon herself to cast shame on Len Armitage in the Sun for 'laughing an' giggling an' spending the money yer should be taking home to yer family,' the reason why, in *Looking Back*, Rosie Craig, conscious of Frank Tattersall's drink problem, says, 'The drink drives out the man and lets the devil in, that's what me mammy used to say.'

Readers of Jo's novels, readers who have met characters as violent as George Kenney in *Her Father's Sins* and Barty Bendall in *Angels Cry Sometimes,* know well enough how powerfully her

'Brookhouse Mills made a daunting and magnificent sight. Like a monstrous stone cake, its grime-covered tiles were the chocolate icing and the long cylindrical chimneys were gigantic candles. The out-pouring smoke snaked through the sky, making weird dark patterns against the bright sunlight which in their very ugliness appeared uniquely beautiful.'

Nobody's Darling

'Eva and Patsy always went by way of Corporation Park; here they could skirt the lawns and enjoy the early blossoms – rhododendrons and roses were already showing their colours… Corporation Park was a haven for Eva; when she felt lonely, and when life seemed to be getting her down she would come into the park and stroll about, or sit and watch the world go by, and it never failed to gladden her heart.'
Love Me Or Leave Me

imagination goes to work to resolve any problems that coloured her life as a child. Back then, she created a little world of her own to get into – 'All the kids in the street were the same, they all had very difficult upbringings,' she says, ringing a chord in the hearts of thousands. It was this aspect of the poverty of life that threatened to give dire emotional significance to the image of Blackburn as a place where 'grimness [is] unmitigated by any natural pleasantness'. It made clear her escape to dream – 'you know, "*When* am I going to have something different? *Why* can't my family have something better?"'

'There was always a need to escape. I used to go up to Corporation Park, and I don't know if the willow tree I used to sit under is still there, but it was huge and old and I used to hide under it. The truant officer would go up the park looking for kids, but he never found me. It was like being *inside* the tree,' Jo continued 'And I would look out so that I could see everything but no-one could see me. I'd watch the world go by. People, animals, and things that were happening; it would all get clocked into my mind. I don't know where I put it all. I was always an outside person because to be inside was to be in a grim place, cold and grim. To be outside was to be free. If

'Corporation Park, a place of great beauty, with a myriad of narrow footpaths and secluded places where a person could sit and lose themselves for as long as they liked... As she hurried along the rhododendron-lined walkways, where every now and then the long swaying tentacles of the many weeping willows dipped and played in the breeze, a soothing sense of peace and love came into Emma's heart.'

Outcast

'The Park was one of the finest in Lancashire with fountains and cliffs, flower-beds and shrubberies, narrow walkways and wide meandering avenues, all overhung with spreading boughs heavy with blossom. There was even a lake, populated by ducks and frequented by each and every one who sought refuge in this delightful oasis. It was incredible but true that here the air smelled sweet and fresh, when only twenty minutes' walk away the atmosphere was choked and sooty, the smoke from the mills leaving its grime and odour on every house, street and thoroughfare in Blackburn.'

Nobody's Darling

'At the bottom of Corporation Park, Tommy stopped. "This is where the posh people live," he said knowledgeably.'

Love Me Or Leave Me

you can get out of yourself, out of the environment which you are in, you are escaping, aren't you?'

When I first started reading Josephine Cox, I couldn't believe that a place called Corporation Park could be anything but, well, municipal and rather dreary. On researching it I discovered little to change my mind, at first. Indeed, its very genesis makes it sound

Above right: *Sunday afternoon, Preston New Road, the middle classes taking a stroll.*

Above & below: *Pleasington (Priory and Old Hall respectively) – one of the enviable middle-class areas fringing the town.*

Below right: *middle-class view of the mill worker colonies.*

formal and hardly the place to which a child from the streets would want to make her escape.

In the 19th century, as more and more mills were built, the middle classes began to put the increasing grimness of the town at arms length, migrating to the fringes (Cherry Tree, Pleasington, Wilpshire, Witton) and taking up residence along the Preston New Road, which offered the ideal vantage point from which to look down on the warren of mill workers' houses in St Paul's Ward, Jo's first playground. The photo below shows the same vantage view today.

In the midst of middle-class Revidge, to the north of Preston

New Road, on November 20, 1857, they opened Corporation Park. Emma Grady was present at the opening, in Jo's novel, *Outcast*.

'I used to hide under this willow tree, it was like being inside it. And I would look out so that I could see everything but no-one could see me. I'd watch the world go by. People, animals, and things that were happening; it would all get clocked into my mind.'

What memories! The mayor and other dignitaries dressed up in the regalia of office and thousands of people from all over the borough assembled to see the park opened. After the opening ceremony, they all surged through the arcuated gateways, some of the women wearing clogs and shawls, others dressed in finer fashion and the men sporting an assortment of flat cloth caps and tall black hats.

The land – 50 acres – had been sold to the town two years earlier by Joseph Feilden (the family had been part owner of the Manor of Blackburn since 1721 and sole owner since the early years of the 19th century). It was originally intended as a middle-class resort. Hundreds of mill workers, laid off during the mass unemployment and famine during the American Civil War (1861-1865), when there was an embargo on raw cotton exports, were employed in improving the park, and it was marked out formally with pristine paths, so that the great and good could see and be seen. It contains two natural lakes – the Can and Big Can, originally Blackburn's earliest reservoirs –

The summit of Corporation Park, where the Crimean guns had stood.

Had Emma visited the summit of the park today and turned round on herself she would have caught sight of The Corporation pub on nearby Revidge Road. It is run by Bernard, one of Jo's brothers.

and, banking steeply to the north, it carried, at one time, two huge artillery guns from the Crimean War (1853-'56) at its highest point.

Corporation Park is a sanctuary for so many of Jo's heroines. For example, in *Love Me Or Leave Me*, Eva and Patsy always go by way of Corporation Park: 'here they could skirt the lawns and enjoy the early blossoms – rhododendrons and roses were already showing their colours...' It was a haven for Eva 'when she felt lonely. When life seemed to be getting her down she would come into the park and stroll about, or sit and watch the world go by, and it never failed to gladden her heart...' In *More Than Riches*, Rosie Selby, whose mother has been killed in a car accident and whose crippled father commits suicide, the Park and specifically the lakeside willow trees, within which Jo had had her den, are a special retreat on cold December mornings. For Kelly Wilson in *Somewhere, Someday*, the park is 'so painfully familiar...the place where she had known so much joy.'

One has to remember the imperviousness of Blackburn to any *sense* of the countryside – in Kelly's brother Michael's words, 'the only countryside I ever saw were the lawns in Corporation Park.' One should also remember Jo's point in *Nobody's Darling* that 'it was incredible but true that here the air smelled sweet and fresh, when only twenty minutes' walk away the atmosphere was choked and sooty, the smoke from the mills leaving its grime and odour on every house, street and thoroughfare in Blackburn.' But also, more than this, we should be clear why the air seemed so fresh to Jo, what it was that she found so attractive in the park. She got inside the willow tree and looked out, she got away in those moments, when getting away – escaping from the grim side of life – was what she needed.

Once I began to stay in Blackburn and visit the park I caught something of what Jo drew from the place. My first visit was during school term time, mid-afternoon, well before the school day was over. I was walking along the tree-covered paths that meander upwards to the summit, no-one else was in sight, when I became aware that I wasn't alone. At first I didn't see anyone, only heard the odd rustling beside me in the secondary layer plantings of rhodos and other shrubs. Then, far ahead of me, someone stepped out of the undergrowth and stepped smartly back in again when he saw me. It became clear that the place was teeming with life and I felt like the truant officer seeking out errant boy and girl life, hiding, as Jo had done, among the boulders and shrub-strewn sides of the hill.

Truth was, Queenie was never at school. Even the Truant Officer had grown tired of fetching her from her various hiding places around Blackburn and there weren't many o' them now that he didn't know about.

Much later, I found myself at the summit, where the Crimean guns

Emma's view as it may be seen today, looking from the summit of Corporation Park over the trees and the town to the snow covered hills beyond. There may be far fewer chimneys than in Emma's day, but even now it offers an escape valve for the people of Blackburn.

had stood, and began taking photographs. While I was there a lad of about 10 or 11 came up to the concrete terrace and sat, some way away from me, for close on half an hour, just looking out across the tops of the trees, over the town. He didn't have a Walkman or a mobile phone. He wasn't even smoking nicotine, he was just gazing at the wonderful view up there, thinking, or perhaps not thinking, clearing his head, cleansing his mind with the kind of un-thinking that sometimes even a young life requires. And I realised that this is much more, indeed quite other, than a municipal park, it is, even today, an escape valve for the kids of Blackburn.

In *Outcast*, Emma Grady is left an orphan and cheated out of her inheritance by her guardian, but after taking the walk I took on that first occasion, she (hopefully like the lad that sat alongside me) got things back into perspective:

Emma felt the urge to visit what had always been her favourite place in the park. This was the very highest point, where the gun turrets from the Crimean War were on display. Emma took the route along the main broad walkway, which would lead her there, via the tall glass-domed conservatories which housed all manner of beautiful plants. As she hurried along the rhododendron-lined walkways, where every now and then the long swaying tentacles of the many weeping willows dipped and played in the breeze, a soothing sense of peace and love came into Emma's heart. Now, rather than grieve for her losses, she gave thanks that at least she still had Manny – her very dear friend and confidante. And here she was, young and healthy, with her whole life ahead of her...

It was a magnificent and awesome sight to behold. From here, she could see over almost the whole of Blackburn town, with its sea of graceful church spires, and, standing tall beside these, as many mill chimneys – the former sending prayers to heaven, and the latter sending up black rancid smoke... Emma saw a curious magic in Blackburn town, and told herself that, in the whole of her life, she would never want to be anywhere else but here.

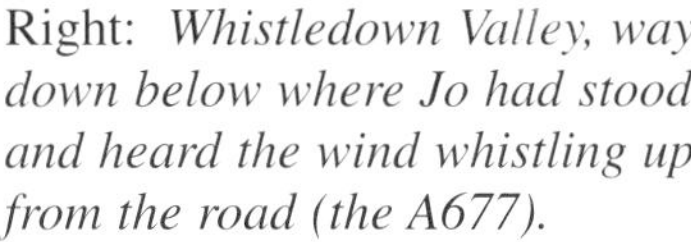

Right: *Whistledown Valley, way down below where Jo had stood and heard the wind whistling up from the road (the A677).*

Below: *the top of the high hill, where Jo stood one day, 'looking right down as far as you can see, and the wind was whistling up from the roadway. That became Whistledown Valley in my novel,* Whistledown Woman.*'*

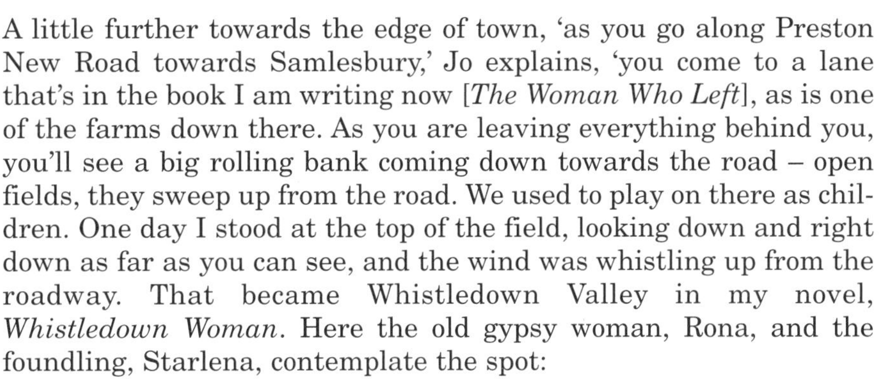

A little further towards the edge of town, 'as you go along Preston New Road towards Samlesbury,' Jo explains, 'you come to a lane that's in the book I am writing now [*The Woman Who Left*], as is one of the farms down there. As you are leaving everything behind you, you'll see a big rolling bank coming down towards the road – open fields, they sweep up from the road. We used to play on there as children. One day I stood at the top of the field, looking down and right down as far as you can see, and the wind was whistling up from the roadway. That became Whistledown Valley in my novel, *Whistledown Woman*. Here the old gypsy woman, Rona, and the foundling, Starlena, contemplate the spot:

From this one vantage point could be seen for miles and miles the valleys and hamlets across an expanse of Lancashire. From the top of the high hill, the green fields fell away in a gently rolling undulation until some four miles in the distance they merged with a small wood. Then they appeared again beyond, and from there they stretched away as far as the eye could see. The whole magnificent panorama

was breathtaking, awing the onlooker into a profound silence... Rona came up to seat herself on the boulder beside the child. The two of them gazed out across the world's expanse and lost themselves in the trembling wonder of it all.

Today, Jo and her husband, Ken, like nothing better than to get in the car and point it in the direction of the moors beyond Blackburn – one of the most beautiful examples of wilderness in all England – and just lose themselves. 'We love it,' Ken says to me. 'There is everything we like. I really mean that, we lose ourselves.'

Says Jo: 'If I had gone there as a child I would never have returned home again.' She insists, 'I love it.' Years ago, Jo didn't know that such beauty exists just 10 miles out of town.

Leaving the smoke behind for the Forest of Bowland.

Ritual

In truth, she was a different girl then, as she will admit: 'I was a *load* of trouble!' She points me to Patsy in *Love Me Or Leave Me*: 'she is actually based on a girl I grew up with. She was trouble, too, exactly the same. This girl was a lot of fun, she was always getting into mischief.'

I encourage the thought: 'Wickedness can be exciting when you're young. That comes across in the books.'

'Oh, God, yes,' she agrees.

'Bringing yourself up on the street,' I say, 'perhaps you were lucky you didn't go wrong?'

'Yes, though not many of my friends went that way. Thinking back to my friends next door or down the street, the ones I used to play with, not many of them went wrong. When I meet them now, most of them have the same values now as they had then. The values that came out of living there. And you looked after each other, you know?'

I wondered whether she, like Queenie, had ever got into trouble with the truancy officer. She admits that one day she did get her comeuppance. Her dad would go off to the Corporation, her mum would go off to Cicely Bridge mill and her brothers and sisters would go off to school, while Jo would go off to Corporation Park, especially if it was Maths. 'I hated the maths teacher, he was a monster! He had red hair, green eyes and a long ruler – and I'd go home with my knuckles all red from his bashing.' Then one day when she decided she wasn't going to school, 'I snuck back and, as usual, hid downstairs for a while in case me mam was to come back or anything. And I heard this noise upstairs. I was really frightened because there shouldn't have been anyone upstairs. It turned out it was my brother Richard! He was playing truant as well!'

I asked Jo how she and her friends on the street had viewed the police.

'I was not afraid of the police,' Jo says. 'They were much more in evidence on the street then, but you knew them as friends. To me they were there to help, though I'll tell you one little story. One night we were playing on the bus station near Henry Street, where they used to park the buses over night, by Blakewater Brook. We used to play in the buses because obviously you could get into them – [they had no motorised passenger doors in those days] – and we used to pretend to be driving and conducting and all that. One time, this policeman saw us and he shouted out and everyone ran, all in different directions. But at that time I had long plaits, and this policeman grabbed hold of me by my plaits! Lifted me off the ground he did and swung me round. I'll never forget that! He made me promise never to go up by the buses again, and then he let me go home with a clip o' the ear. When I got home, I told me mam, and *she* gave me a clip o' the ear! So, you see, they were friends, part of the community.'

Stories like that remind us that whatever happened at home, whatever the grim realities of the street, *fun was had*. And largely it was safe fun. Believing somewhere deep inside that Blackburn was theirs, earned by the sweat of their forebears' labours, Jo and her friends ran like fauns in some magic, mythic, lantern-lit land. They didn't just happen to be there, they were part of the place, as surely as the cobbles that dug deep into the street, and every so often a community event came along to prove it.

'Jazz Band Night was a ritual every year,' recalls Jo. 'In Blackburn and across Preston and Darwen, it was a ritual, though we were talking about it in the pub the other day and some of the people who come from further out hadn't heard of it. We'd put our hands up the chimney and cover them in soot and blacken ourselves! Everything had to be covered. You could only see the whites of our eyes. Then you'd get anything that made a noise, the old pans, you'd get a stick and beat the pans. Outside the pub you'd go, and the men would come out drunk. They'd give you more money if they were drunk.'

I mention the famously huge annual Blackburn bonfire. In the 1930s, I had been told, it was held in the large back yard of the Dog Inn in Revidge, but Jo remembers it on an open area down in the centre of town by Blakewater Bridge (before the Blakewater was culverted in the

'The bobbies!' Maisie's loud fearful whisper sent a shiver through the girl. 'Cissie Armstrong. . . may Gawd help yer if you've fetched the police to this door.' ... 'I didn't do it, Mam!' she cried fearfully.' Don't Cry Alone
'I was not afraid of the police,' Jo says. 'They were much more in evidence on the street then, but you knew them as friends.'

1960s) – 'really where the covered shopping area is today.' It is featured in *Angels Cry Sometimes:*

When Blackburn Town Hall officials put on the celebrations for the annual bonfire, they really meant business. It seemed to Marcia that every nook and cranny was bursting at the seams. There were more people here than she could ever remember before, and more vendors of all descriptions were peddling their wares, or calling out for eager members of the milling crowd to 'Come and have a go!' There were shooting-ranges; catch-a-goldfish stall, candy-floss and toffee-apple kiosks; roll-a-penny chutes, and many more...

Right in the very centre stood the bonfire. No ordinary bonfire this! It was all of twenty feet high and more, with a base circumference which would easily have swallowed the downstairs area of Grandma Fletcher's little terraced house. If you stretched your neck up into the night, to look beyond the mountain of timber, rags, paper, furniture and anything else that would produce a crackling flame, you would be rewarded by the awesome sight of Guy Fawkes. A monstrous creature, seated in a great wooden armchair, he claimed pride of place right on the very highest plateau. From there, he could survey the gathering admirers below...

That very evening the big bonfire would be lit

and, following the tradition which had evolved over many years, it would draw great numbers of folks hereabouts, from their cosy firesides. It would light up the skies over Lancashire like some gigantic fiery beacon.

The memory of it sparks the true story of the horsehair sofa that appears in the same novel: 'My mam had this black horsehair settee. You'd sit on it and it would prick your legs, and you'd leap up off it because it was pricking you. She used to say, "Eee I'd luv a nice three-piece suite, you know? Two armchairs, one for me and one for yer dad." And then Bernard came in the night before bonfire night and said he'd just seen two seats and a settee on the bonfire. Guy Fawkes was sitting on one of the armchairs on top of the bonfire. So, when mam and dad had gone to bed, we snuck out, all of us, and we took our horsehair settee and changed it for the three-piece suite on the fire. It was the most ghastly three-piece suite you have ever seen – green with yellow flowers! I can see it still. In the morning, we all got down before her and hid behind the settee to see how she would react. She opened the door, and stood there and stared at it for ages. As we popped out from behind the settee she looked at us and said, "Wor the bloody hell did you get that?!" She knew we'd been up to something no good, but she loved it.'

The tiny parlour was filled with ugliness. All the good furniture that had belonged to old Mrs Bendall had either fallen to bits, or had been sold to keep the food cupboards replenished. The heavy brown sideboard that stood against the window, the rocking-chair in which she sat, the big square table and the few stand-chairs around it, were pieces that had been rescued at various times from local bonfires and second-hand shops, where better-off families had discarded them. The black horsehair settee, grotesque in appearance, but clean and functional, had been deftly removed one dark night from the bandaged feet of a bright Guy Fawkes destined, like the furniture, to be reduced to ashes. The Bendall children, unknown to Marcia, had spirited the settee away, cleaned and dusted it, then set it out in the parlour as a surprise treat for their Mam, who displayed the gratitude and enthusiasm that the occasion warranted. Marcia minded very much having to accept other people's cast-offs. But no one knew any better than she did that pride was a luxury she could not afford.

Blackburn was not a prime target of the Luftwaffe during World War II. In fact, in 1939, children from Manchester had been evacuated to the town for their safety. There were only three instances of bombs falling on the town – one in Bennington Street, some way south of the town centre, another at Whitekirk, again away from the centre (to the north east), and the other very centrally, in Ainsworth Street, close to the market square and Henry Street. It fell just before midnight on August 31, 1940. The damage caused by this bomb provided the amphitheatre for Jo's public storytelling, which began after an English teacher at school had taken a particular interest in her.

'I didn't like school,' stresses Jo. 'In fact, I *hated* it, except for English.'

Hearing old Snake-tongue, as the kids called Miss Jackson, the English teacher, reading from Dickens' *Oliver Twist*, a story inspired by the author's own bleak childhood, Jo was mesmerised. 'I thought, "That could be me. Here's this boy, scruffy and ragged like me," Oliver Twist was someone I could relate to. His going to the workhouse brought back memories because every time my mother had a baby we were sent to a council home.'

Like Queenie, Jo was her 'own lass' from a very early age, sensitive to the needs of her mother and quick to take control of a situation, even though she had an older sister, Winifred, and two older brothers, James (nicknamed Sonny because he was always smiling) and Joseph. 'When we were put in the council home, when mam had to go to hospital to have a baby and there was no-one to look after us, I was always the one – even though I was fourth in line – who would plead with the matron, "Please don't separate us," and I'd cry and get all upset, and they never did.' The memory recalls the practice, prevalent even in the 20th century, of segregating the sexes for admission to the workhouse, the men to one side, women to the other.

'I started charging the kids a penny each to sit on the bomb rubble while I told them stories. If any didn't have a penny, I'd kick 'em out,' Jo recalls.

'I began to make up stories about my grandad and his dog, about friends and family. Then, on Fridays after school, I started charging the other kids a penny each to sit on the bomb rubble in the street while I told them stories. If any turned up to listen and didn't have a penny, I'd kick 'em out. All the week I'd be thinking, "What stories shall I tell?" Sometimes I would go to my grandad's and he'd sit me on his knee and tell me magical stories, and I'd tell them to my friends, but I'd also make up new adventures.'

The pennies ended up in the gas meter at home or paid for a loaf of bread. Then one day, when Jo was 11, there was a competition at St Anne's in which everyone had to write a story about someone they knew. Jo wrote one about her grandad and his dog and won the prize – a pencil and writing case. 'I stood on the stage while Miss Jackson told the school, "One day the whole world will read Josephine's stories." And something happened inside me. That is *it*! I had decided that I wanted to write my stories and that I wanted everyone to read them.'

Old Snake-tongue appeared in Jo's first book, *Her Father's Sins*, and her erstwhile teacher was not amused. 'She came to my first signing session and she was not happy!' recalls Jo. 'You see, she hadn't known that the kids called her Snake-tongue until I put it in the book! Can you believe that? And I had thought she was dead!' One can appreciate Jo's shock when she found out that she was very much alive...

St Anne's, the class of '54. 'I didn't like school,' stresses Jo. 'In fact, I hated it, except for English.'

Today, under distinct duress and displaying a heavy frown, Queenie had to suffer Miss Jackson, or Snake-Tongue as she was better known. Her tight weasel-face and sneck mouth drove the children into themselves, producing mountainous resentment and squashing any desire to learn. Miss Snake-Tongue Jackson hadn't a friend in the world. She was a pain, a moan, a blind mouth that spouted nothing but horrors. Queenie hated her, and when hometime bell clattered she was off to the safe and comfortable company of Auntie Biddy. Today, after having a warm all-over wash in the tin bath before the fire, and gulping down a bowl filled with dumpling stew, Queenie had helped to fold the day's considerable pile of washing. Auntie Biddy had watched her yawning. 'Sleepy are you, lass?' she'd asked gently. Queenie told her with fervent conviction that it was only that rotten school and Snake-Tongue as made her tired. Even so, she didn't put up too much of an argument when Auntie Biddy quietly but firmly ushered her up to bed.

And so life went on. The sounds of Blackburn filled the air from early dawn to gas-lamp lighting. Some men commandeered a piece of wasteland for a small plot of land and a pigeon coop, and for others, after the pubs, in order of importance, came Blackburn Rovers, the betting-shops, picture-houses and slipper-baths; 'although rather than waste sixpence on a tub of hot water at the slipper-baths, the man of the house would much rather spend it "wisely" on a swig of healthy ale.'

These slipper baths interested me. Jo had no idea how the public baths came to be so

The usual bathing ritual was to bring in the tin bath from the nail on the backyard wall.

Belper Street swimming baths. 'We went to the swimming baths with the school and once I nearly drowned. After that I stayed well away from swimming pools. I suppose it was when I was about nine. I was always a tomboy and there were three diving boards. I couldn't swim, but I got right up onto the top diving board, stood there as if I was going to dive with my arms outstretched and some teenager pushed me. The last thing I remember was seeing all these legs under the water and I was shouting Mummy, Mummy, and taking all the water in. Then the next thing I knew I was on the side and the water shooting out of my mouth. To this day I will not go out of my depth.'

named. They were at the bottom of Peter Street, and presumably disappeared in the 1960s in the drastic Larkhill re-development. The usual bathing ritual was to bring in the tin bath from the nail on the backyard wall; then, by surrounding it with stand-chairs covered with towels or sheets, some semblance of privacy could be gained. But for a girl just reaching her double years, and passing through that self-conscious period, it was less than satisfactory, which is why Marcia, in *Angels Cry Sometimes*, suggests that Polly's increasing embarrassment might be diminished in the comparative luxury of the *slipper baths*, housed in the centre of town, in the Municipal Buildings.

However, as Polly discovers to her bitter shame, the point about the slipper baths is, 'You almost always had to share! And you didn't know who you were going to be sharing with!' Jo recalls. 'Children would share with children obviously, but if it was full up and it was sixpence to have a bath they would charge you threepence and you had to share. And, you know, you could be sharing with anybody!' Polly has to share and Jo leaves us in no doubt that she herself must surely have experienced the same embarrassment at about the same age:

A visit to the baths was a rare treat, and though the youngsters didn't always appreciate the luxury of a real bath and hot water from a tap, the grown-ups relished the opportunity. A bathroom, or even an indoor toilet, were not facilities afforded to the likes of Marcia's family or indeed to the vast majority of Blackburn's inhabitants...

After seeing Florence and young Barty safely to the picture house, Marcia and Polly made their way to the slipper baths. Saturday morning was a particularly busy time, and Marcia was not surprised to see a considerable queue. People of all ages and various sizes and shapes waited patiently for the church clock to strike ten, when the heavy wooden doors would be opened, and the bathers allowed in. Meanwhile, there was still no sign of Polly's friend Bridget Revine.

The Rialto in Penny Street, where young Barty and Florence repaired, was the largest cinema in Blackburn in Jo's day.

'I'll just wander to the edge of Market Square, Mam... to see if she's coming.' Polly was growing increasingly anxious.

'All right then, but you'll not have to be long, lass...'

'It's all right Mam, there's still time.'

...Within five minutes of the doors being opened, Marcia and Polly, who had had no luck in locating Bridget, were being ushered into their separate cubicles. It was an unusually busy morning but the queue was dealt with rapidly. Entrance money had been taken, towels supplied, and cubicles issued with surprising speed and efficiency.

'Numbers six and seven lasses. Be as quick as you can, 'cause we're right pushed this morning, as you can see! Might even need to double up with you young 'uns later on...' The friendly barrel-shaped woman addressed herself to Polly, before waddling quickly away to collect another bather.

Polly pushed open the door to the cubicle. 'Oh Mam! I don't want nobody sharing,' she told Marcia sulkily.

'I'm sure they'll manage without asking you to share, lass,' Marcia assured her, 'so stop your moithering, an' get inside. Go on,' she urged the hesitant girl.

After seeing Polly into her cubicle, Marcia thankfully stepped inside No. 7. Crossing over to the big white bath, she ran her hand lovingly over its smooth surface, letting her fingers travel slowly up to the taps. Revelling in the rare luxury of it all, Marcia savoured the pleasure which rippled through her senses. She caressed the walls, the hand-basin, towel rail...in fact, everything that was unfamiliar and scarce in her own needy world. Eventually, putting the bath plug in, Marcia turned the taps on, letting her small measure of soap slither into the bath before testing the water for the correct temperature. Then, as the warm steaming liquid tumbled into the bath, she began to unclothe herself, impatient to immerse herself into the gathering foam. With slow deliberation, she lowered herself into the warm sudsy water, sighing with pleasure as it lapped and caressed against her nakedness.

Outside, Bridget had reached the head of the

queue. She had brought her own soap and towel. 'Just a ticket please,' she asked, as she handed the coppers over.

The cashier peered at her through tiny rimless spectacles, before turning to the barrel-shaped lady. 'Have we got any young 'uns in, Mabel?' she asked.

'Aye. We've got a couple o' lasses... one in 6, and one in 19.'

'Six is the biggest one, I think,' the cashier observed, then noticing the disappointed expression on Bridget's face, she asked her, 'You don't mind sharing do you lass? I'm afeared it's all we've got till the next session.'

'No, that's all right missus. I've had to share before,' Bridget confessed.

'Right then. Number 6 Mabel,' she said as she nodded smartly to the barrel-shaped woman, who in turn indicated to Bridget that she wanted her to follow.

Marcia, deeply immersed in the bath water, wasn't quite sure whether the insistent tapping was at her door. She slid herself up in the water, listening with sharper attention. The voice was easily recognisable as that of the barrel-shaped woman, but Marcia quickly contented herself that it was not directed at her.

'Open the door. You'll have to share with this lassie out here. We've got no more cubicles left this session,' came the instruction.

Chances are that Florence and Barty had enjoyed themselves rather more at the Rialto picture house, where, from the 1920s, a Saturday matinee was shown, originally for the payment of two empty 2lb jam jars. For wannabe teenagers, however, like Polly or, indeed, Jo, the nearest you got to a groove was Teddy's shop, a cross between an ancient herbalist's and a '50s' milk bar, run by a 'twisted dwarf figure with huge pink eyes and a bald head', who knew how to cure everything from a toe-ache to a broken heart. It is still there today, on King Street. 'He would sell you a pennyworth of sarsaparilla. Three of you would just sit there, and you'd have a penny which you would go and earn. Sarsaparilla was a forerunner to Coca Cola.' Jo featured the tiny place in her first novel:

It was only a ten-minute walk to Teddy's shop, off the High Street and down a cobbled alley. Teddy was a twisted dwarfed figure, with huge pink eyes and a bald head. His little shop, well known throughout Blackburn, sold the finest herbs, spices, Woodbines and snuff. It was a delightfully quaint old shop, with layers of deep shelves from floor to ceiling. Each shelf was crammed with jars containing green rosemary, black liquorice, wood sticks, brown snuff, pink and yellow barley-twists and hundreds of other colourful herbs and remedies of all shape and description. It was said that he knew how to cure everything from a toe-ache to a broken heart.

The deep glass-fronted counter where you paid your purchases was filled with spacious tubs of different-coloured Khali, a kind of fizzy sherbet powder; along the floor against every wall stood enormous stone bottles of sarsaparilla; a delicious tar-coloured liquid which stung your nose and brought tears to your eyes. A long narrow glass of sarsaparilla was a real treat and was usually drunk in comfort and leisure on the 'staying seat'. The staying seat was tucked away out of sight behind a green curtain. Anyone fancying a measure of sarsaparilla just sat themselves down on it, and waited for Teddy to serve them.

Then, every Easter came the fair, not just any fair. They held it on the old market square, and it had a long, well-tried pedigree. For instance, in 1849, writes Derek Beattie in the town's most authoritative history – *Blackburn: The Development of a Lancashire Cotton Town*, the 'main attraction was a large-headed girl, rabbit-eyed children and a lady giant... Boxing, ring tossing, popgun shooting, wheels of fortune and sword swallowing made up a few of the sideshows.'

'The Fair! Mam! I can 'ear the fair! I can smell the baked tatties!' Young Barty's feet barely touched the ground, and his little flat cap bobbed about excitedly as he hopped and jumped, ears straining, towards the tinny rhythmic tones wafting towards them on the breeze. In that miraculous way that children have, young Barty had opted to put the distasteful memories of the earlier scene out of his mind; 'Oh go on Mam! Please,' he insisted, 'please let me 'ave a ride on the 'orses.'

Florence hurried to keep up. 'Yes, and can we all have roasted chestnuts?' she pleaded.

'We'll see,' Marcia laughed...

As the family turned the corner on to Ainsworth

Street, the whole colourful scene lay before them like the setting on a stage, only this was real!

The music filled Marcia's soul with joy as she perused the busy scene. It seemed as if the whole world and his friend were here to enjoy the festivities. The area was decked from one end to the other with twinkling lights and from every corner there came the shouts of excited stall-holders clamouring for attention. There was no official entrance as such, but the positioning of stalls and stages dictated points of access, and flanking every path colourful enterprising characters had set up their varied diversions. At the junction where the stalls split away to either side, a little wizened man had placed his barrel organ in a shrewd position, so that anyone emerging from Ainsworth Street had no choice but to pass him before reaching the centre of activity.'

'Everybody loved the fair,' agreed Jo. 'There was a woman who used to come with it, she had her own caravan and a daughter who was fifteen when my sister was about twelve and I was about ten, and she would give us clothes and shoes and great big earrings and things, and we'd dress up. They were long – it was silly really, they were too grown up for us, but we loved them and we'd go round in them. Things you never want to forget. The fair was magic, magic!'

I asked whether her family could afford to go on the rides. 'We used to *work* on the rides. We used to collect the money. It could be quite dangerous. You know the caterpillar thing that goes up and down? My brothers used to collect the money there. Myself and my sister Winifred used to work on the hoopla, collecting the money.' This must be why she lets Polly win on the hoopla in *Angels Cry Sometimes*, knowing how unusual a event winning on the hoopla is: ''Ere, 'ave you done this afore?' demands the woman working on the stall that night, looking for an excuse not to pay out.

'We got very friendly with the people who owned the fair and the stalls,' Jo told me. 'They were gypsy characters, tough they were. You'd see many a fight, bare knuckles.' I mention *Looking Back*, the novel in which Alfie, Molly's Tattersall's boyfriend, is a bare knuckle boxer. 'When I saw them fighting behind the fair on the spare ground,' says Jo, 'they would knock hell out of each other. And apparently they use to do this fighting everywhere and I looked into it. Ireland was very well known for it. They would do this not just for play, but for real, really going at each other.' It is in *Looking Back* that we get inside the mind of one of these fairground people, before tragedy strikes. 'The waltzers was my favourite,' says Jo, 'still is.'

It was the third time Lottie had been on the Waltzer. 'So you've money to burn, have you?' The tall, gangly young man collected her payment, at the same time leaning over her shoulder and looking her in the eye. 'Is it the sight of me that thrills you, or is it the thrill of the ride?'

'Huh!' Lottie had achieved what she wanted. At last she had caught his

'"The Fair! Mam! I can 'ear the fair! I can smell the baked tatties!" Young Barty's feet barely touched the ground.'
Angels Cry Sometimes

'The place was thronging with people, mostly young, mostly screaming on the rides, or strolling arm-in-arm, or pressed up against some stationary object, frantically fumbling each other. The fairground did that to people... ' Looking Back

eye. 'Got a high opinion of yerself, ain't yer?' Though the insult was meant, her laughing eyes told another story.

'Cheeky devil!' Brash and confident, he smiled into her face, his hand touching her hair, making her shiver with delight. When Lottie smiled back, his sharp eyes caught sight of the notes protruding from her jacket pocket. 'Where did you get all that money, eh?' Now he was even more interested.

Stuffing the notes out of sight, Lottie gave him a wary glance. 'I earned it, what d'yer think?'

He quickly changed tactics. 'None o' my business,' he slyly apologised, stroking his hand over her shoulder. 'Only you shouldn't be walking about with all that cash on you, especially like that...' he flicked her pocket '...where any Tom, Dick or Harry can see it. There's some artful buggers round this fairground, and I should know.' 'Cos I'm one of them, he thought, though he wasn't about to tell her that – at least, not until he'd got what he wanted out of the silly bitch.

'I can take care of myself!'

'We used to work on the rides. We used to collect the money. It could be quite dangerous. You know the caterpillar thing that goes up and down? My brothers used to collect the money there. Myself and my sister Winifred used to work on the hoopla, collecting the money.'

'The Waltzer was the most popular ride on the fair. Great iron buckets of colour and speed... Head down and eyes intent on the riders, Dave hopped from one bucket to the next, collecting the money and dropping it into the pouch round his waist. Now the Waltzer was gaining speed and he had no time to look up.' Looking Back

He grinned. 'I'm sure you can.' A thought occurred to him. ''Ere! I'm no cradle-snatcher! How old are you?' It was no matter. He had her in his sights and was not about to let her loose.

'I'm eighteen.'

'Liar.' Snaking out his tongue, he licked her on the neck, making her giggle. 'You're never eighteen!'

'All right, I'm sixteen. Why d'you want to know?' Lies became easier the more you told them.

Tantalisingly, he licked the inside of her ear and said huskily, 'If I'm about to take you to bed, I need to know if you're old enough.'

'What makes you think I want to go to bed with you?'

For a brief moment her coy manner had him foxed, then she smiled up at him and he knew he had her. 'Oh, you want me all right,' he whispered. 'I can always tell.'

'I'm not one of your easy girls!' Anger coloured her face.

'Aye aye – looks like I've got a fiery one here. But that's all right – it's more fun.' He laughed, a low, sarcastic sound that should have warned her. Instead, she was excited.

'Nobody's managed to tame me yet,' she boasted.

'I'll bring you to heel my girl, given time.'

Lottie is in fact only 15 at the time of this seduction, which leads to terrible things. Elsewhere the story impinges a great deal on Jo's life. For example, Lottie's elder sister, Molly, having seen their mother, Amy, manage her brood – 'four little 'uns and the two older girls...might as well be sixty, the way they drive me to despair' – tells her boyfriend Alfie that she would be happy to settle for only two children when they get married. We see, too, that Amy's husband, Frank, drinks away the wages on a Friday night – 'So what! If I'm drunk it's my money I'm spending, not yourn.' But at the fairground in *Angels Cry Sometimes*, for one time only, we see one of these strong but beleaguered, loving but mistreated, matriarchal figures, Marcia Bendall, expressing with rare sensitivity the nature of the burden these women carry, their sorrow, if you like. Marcia's husband, Barty, who shares many of the characteristics of Jo's father in real life, has died. Little Ada Humble's husband, Toby, has likewise come to grief, in his case on his Saucy-Sally, the huge iron bike he would ride unsteadily back home from the pub when he had one too many. So there was emotion in the air that night. But what we see, in fact, cuts deeper than the sadness Marcia and Ada feel about their men folk. It seems to hark farther back to that heroic yet tragic element in northern working class culture, which threaded the people of this area together. It was certainly spontaneous enough to surprise them all:

'My most vivid memory of the fair,' explained Jo, 'was this big generator wagon. The front of the wagon dropped down, so it was like a big shop, and they used to sell things from it, but now and again they would have someone singing in there, singing over a tannoy. That was where me mam sang one time. She chose 'Danny Boy'. She used to love singing but she only did it the once in public. She was a shy person, but a very lovely looking lady – long dark hair, big dark eyes. I remember all us kids were down there and there had been a man singing and it was absolutely beautiful. But then, on this particular night, my mam got up and sang. I couldn't believe it, I was so proud. Never had she had a chance to express it. We were mesmerised.'

The song became a story, and the story breathed life, and Marcia's voice was never more magnificent. For a few precious moments time rolled back and once again, each heart knew the joy of embracing a loved one. They knew also the despair when one was taken.

There was nary a sound from the four hundred-strong audience. Even the stall-holders and fair-folks had brought their churning machinery to a halt... Marcia's caressing words bathed the cool night in a soft gentle warmth, weaving a magic spell...[and] when the song drew to a close, the crowd stood transfixed. Then, of a sudden, the silence was broken. The cheers that had caught in the choking fullness of their throats broke through in waves of shouts and whistles, all praising Marcia and all wanting more.

'God bless you lass.'

2 STRATAGEM & STRIFE

In order to understand the elements of working class culture that thread the people of this area together – the warp and weft with which Josephine Cox weaves her spell – we must go back to a time when Derwent Street, where she was born, was an undisturbed, green and pleasant strip of land.

As I wrote in the *Prologue*, peasants living in this area before Blackburn began its 19th-century industrial sprawl, had, for hundreds of years, been engaged in the business of weaving cloth. They were part of a tradition – a rural, not an urban, tradition – that went back centuries. It was other than a job, it was a way of life, indeed it was a whole unconscious philosophy of life, a way of surviving in the countryside, free from bondage to an employer. Theirs was a tradition not only in the sense of craft customs and the skills of spinning and weaving (though they were of course part of it), but also in the sense of beliefs and the very *character* of life. So important was this tradition that when the revolution swept it aside, there arose a requiem to it, an inspired outpouring of Blackburn poets, loom workers and the like, who would recite their works at a spot on Blakeley (now Blakey) Moor in the centre of town.

The story of the industrial revolution, which enticed these people to de-camp from the countryside into the town, thereby participating in the biggest social change Britain has ever seen, is the story of how their time-honoured tradition was both exploited and transformed and how a certain dogged moral, even spiritual, dimension of it enabled the weavers and spinners to survive the horrors that lay in store, their struggle setting the stage for a 20th-century culture of human rights.

The craft way of life was, originally, as close to nature as farming. The natural environment – the local soft water and damp climate –

He put his picks in straight an' fair,
An' ne'er his duty shirk'd;
No mooter fell to Peter's share
Fro' ony sooart he werk'd
Th' owd putter-eawt could trust him weel,
An' when t'brisk times wer gone,
Peter could use his troddle heel,
An' mek a potterin' on...

Theirs was a tradition not only in the sense of craft customs and the skills of spinning and weaving (though they were of course part of it), but also in the sense of beliefs and the very character of life.

favoured it; it was undertaken in the countryside; and it dovetailed with living off the land. At first, spinning and weaving were a way to eke out incomes from land-based labours, especially during the barren winter months. The crafts were undertaken at home, the finished material sent from outlying villages by packhorse and wagon into the town to be sold. The cotton and linen yarns were spun on a simple treadle- or hand-powered spinning wheel, and the yarn was woven into cloth on a hand loom. Long hours were spent in the process and it was physical work. Generally, the men of the household would do the weaving, the women the spinning.

Spinning a continuous, twisted strand of natural cotton fibres, each of which is short and about as fine as a human hair, spinning a yarn as we say, is probably as old as the art of story-telling itself – Indian and Egyptian records of the craft take us back to 3,000 BC – and the pun is not arbitrary. There has long been an association between looms and literature. I have already mentioned the Blackburn poets, central to whose work is the poetic celebration of the hand-loom weaver tradition, but Blackburn is not the only town to produce weaver poets: in the same century Longfellow found the same in 'Nuremberg', where the 'flowers of poesy bloom...in the tissues of the loom.'

What is noticeable is the moral vein that these poets let in the characterisation of the weaving tradition, and it is that vein on which we will see the industrial revolution going to work. 'Owd Peter', Henry Yates's portrait of an old hand-loom weaver, is a man honest and proud to his core –

Hand-loom weavers cottages at Ribchester.

Owd Peter wer a gradely mon,
  As ever breathed a pray'r;
His record stood abeawt A1,
  For wod were reet an' square...

He put his picks in straight an' fair,
  An' ne'er his duty shirk'd;
No mooter fell to Peter's share
  Fro' ony sooart he werk'd
Th' owd putter-eawt could trust him weel,
  An' when t'brisk times wer gone,
Peter could use his troddle heel,
  An' mek a potterin' on...

Joseph Hodgson, born in 1783, was another Blackburn weaver and poet, as was Richard Dugdale, a parish apprentice, born around 1790, who never had a day's schooling in his life and became known as 'the bard of Ribblesdale'. In *Poets & Poetry of Blackburn*, published in 1902, George Hull, himself a poet of the town, puts the very unusual number of men writing and reciting poetry in Blackburn down to the depth of need for imaginative escape from 'the smoke and smudge of the factory and the foundry,' and he points to 'those beauties of nature which may be found so plentifully scattered around him, as soon as he has climbed any of the hills that encircle the town itself.'

Certainly these poets are inspired by beauty. There are poems that extol the natural beauty of the nearby countryside, and there are poems like those of hand-loom weaver turned factory operative John Baron that bewail the loss of beauty in Blackburn itself. But their point is the *loss* of beauty, as the revolution gathers pace

Wild geese fly up the Ribble to Ribchester, one of a few hand-loom weaving towns where the tradition survived even as late as 1890.

and the weavers and spinners are drawn by need to the increasingly industrialised town, and looking back to a time in the town itself when it was 'blessed by many a green nook'.

The industrial revolution squeezed nature out of the town with Judgement-Day finality. As Jo wrote in *Angels Cry Sometimes* of the neighbourhood of her home in Henry street: 'There were no seasonal changes, each day being a continuation of the day before, and even the birds sought brighter climates.'

But the loss of beauty that these poets mourn is not only in nature. They are looking with sadness to an era that is passing before their very eyes, to a rural tradition in transit, to an idyll that the industrial revolution is sweeping away, to the autonomous, rurally-based lifestyle of the independent hand-loomer and to deep-rooted values that will, over the next 150 years, be transformed by the urban factory system, the mill masters' greed and the conditions they impose. They are looking back, in effect, to the innocent 'childhood' of Blackburn's history.

Richard Rawcliffe was born in Ribchester in 1839, where he became a hand-loom weaver before moving the few miles to

George Hull saw the late 18th and 19th-century craftsman's 'strong love of nature' as 'the first germs of that poetic genius with which Blackburn has been so richly dowered.' There developed a poetic tradition that celebrated the beauty of the nearby countryside and the 'truth' of the weaver and spinners' way of life up in the hills around Blackburn. These poets were ordinary craftsmen, who had been displaced by the revolution and had discovered, in their new urban condition, that rural beauty signals more than simply a pretty scene.

Four-fifths of the nation lived in villages or small towns in 1801, but by 1901 three-quarters lived in cities or large industrial towns like Blackburn. That was the nature of the immense change wrought by the industrial revolution. Whether or not many of those who left the country for their new urban life of uniformity and exploitation in the Blackburn mill colonies would admit that they had been happier in the country, where many had been very poor, is not known, but the Blackburn poets do lament the loss of freedom and independence inherent in the old life of rural seclusion and immutability.

Blackburn to work on a power loom, eventually becoming an overlooker. First, in Rawcliffe's 'Idylls by the Hearth', comes tradition in sweet, rural process:

Another weary day had fled, –
The fire was burning low and red;
'Twas late, my Ruth and babes in bed
  Were soundly sleeping.

Outside the door the wintry rain,
Came tapping at the window pane;
When calmly, softly, to my brain
  Sweet thoughts came creeping.

The mouser watched beside the hole;
The cinders one by one did fall,
And darkly on the kitchen wall
  Were shadows flitting;
And many an old familiar face,

Among the cinders I did trace,
While I, in my accustomed place,
In thought was sitting....

The Blackburn poets were hard working men, and there were lots of them, which is surprising. Would one not have expected hard men such as these tacklers to have despised the form as esoteric?

The hand-loom weaver is in tune and in time with the rural scene around him. There is complete empathy, and from nature herself he draws the deep-truth values that characterise the tradition that he is living, values which, in the following extract, bestow on him the title of *working-class hero*, an epithet that would endure in spite of the revolution and be the 20th-century working-class rallying call:

...The man who glories in the right: –
In honest toil 'neath virtue's wing:
He struggles hard from morn till night,
And calmly bears affliction's sting
To get the needful things of life,
And nobly thus he battles through
The falls and bruises of the strife:
Methinks that man's a hero too.

extract from 'Heroes'

The Blackburn poets were hard working men, and there were lots of them, which is surprising. Would one not have expected hard men such as these to have despised the form as esoteric? Not if one is to believe J C Prince, who was one of them:

If, 'mid the world's rude shock and strife,
Thou hast no sense of things divine,
No longing for the holier life, –
Oh, what a priceless loss is thine!

There were tradesmen, too, like Robert Clemesha, a grocer and tea dealer who stored his verses 'among his pepper an' his 'bacco an' his snuff' in his shop on King William Street. Some of these poets were published in book form, others published themselves on broadsheets, selling them wherever they went. John Charlton, a cobbler also living close to the Market Place, railed in his poetry against the exploitation of the working man and spread his works around the local pubs. Liking a drink, he also 'furnished fun and amusement for many a bar-parlour' with his favourite songs, such as 'The Mayor of Mellor', 'Yer Margit's Sister', 'The Poet's Prince', and raised a glass or two with 'The Miser Landlord' and 'The Brewer's Coachman'.

It might have served Jo as a child to have alluded to Charlton when her father dismissed her own literary aspirations: 'When he came home from a hard day's work,' she told me, 'the last thing he wanted to hear was any of my airy-fairy nonsense.' A century earlier it was exactly what the hard working, hard drinking

As you approach the area of Pendle Hill today there is still the aura of sorcery in the air. In the 17th century, spinning was not the only craft able to claim continuity with a rural culture thousands of years old.

Then, in the 18th-century, the Age of Reason swept superstition aside and prepared the people of Lancashire for two centuries of invention, materialism and entrepreneurship, the like of which the world had never seen and could not have imagined.

Blackburn man *did* want to hear. In a very real sense, Jo belongs to this tradition. A respect for the truth-divining form of poetry, and in particular for its Romantic propensities, may have been encouraged in Blackburn by a lingering sense of the pantheistic superstitions common in earlier times. For, in the 17th century, spinning was not the only craft able to claim continuity with a rural culture thousands of years old.

On March 18, 1612, on the road to Colne, a woman called Alison Device, native of the Forest of Pendle, close to what is the M65 north-eastern approach to Blackburn today, begged for some pins from a pedlar and was refused. Device cursed the man, apparently paralysing him. Brought to account, the woman confessed to practising witchcraft, implicating her mother, Elizabeth Southern, and another local, Anne Whittle. As these women were known respectively as Old Mother Demdike and Old Mother Chattox, it might seem a fair bet that they were indeed witches, and sure enough tales of their turning ale sour at the inn at Higham and using a clay doll to bewitch the landlord's son, causing his death, were soon widespread.

Later it emerged that each of the two women had a following at odds with the other's, the son-in-law of one of them paying the other old woman in meal for his own protection, and the two witches vying with each other to claim responsibility for any atrocities that occurred in the area.

Alison Device was committed for trial at the Lancaster Assizes, along with the two dames and Anne Redfern, Anne Whittle's daughter, all of them held at Lancaster castle. Within a week of their committal, as Thomas Potts, Clerk of the Assize Court, recorded at the time, 'at Malkin Tower in the Forest of Pendle, upon a good-fryday,' there gathered together 'all the most dangerous and wicked and damnable witches in the country, far and near... In their great assemble it was decreed that M. Covell by reason of his office [he was the gaoler at Lancaster Castle] shall be slain before the next Assizes, the Castle of Lancaster to be blown up.' Malkin Tower is believed to have been on Blacko Hill, to the east of the region, some of those alleged to have participated in this meeting were carted off to Lancaster Castle too.

In total, nineteen people were imprisoned at Lancaster, charged with practising witchcraft. Eight came from a village called Samlesbury, by what is now the A677 north-western approach to Blackburn, although only three of these so-called Samlesbury witches were actually brought to trial, namely Jennet and Ellen Brierley and Jane Southworth. Their accuser was 14-year-old Grace Sowerbutts, Ellen Brierley's granddaughter. The charge was that the women had conspired by 'witchcrafts, enchantments, charms and sorceries,' at times in the guise of a black dog, to cause Grace's body to become 'wasted and consumed'. The full text of Grace's testimony is extraordinary, violent and very strange.

In the case against Jane Southworth, however, the Court perceived a pretext for the charge

Pendle Hill in the Forest of Pendle where 'upon a good-fryday,' there gathered together 'all the most dangerous and wicked and damnable witches in the country, far and near. . .' Nine of the Pendle witches and their accomplices were hanged.

against her in the then current political upheaval in the established Church. She was the daughter of Sir Richard Sherburne of Stonyhurst, home today to the well-known Roman Catholic public school, a few miles north of Blackburn. She was also the widow of the grandson of Sir John Southworth, the 16th-century lord of the manor of Samlesbury, whose strong Catholic beliefs and allegiances had made him a front line supporter of Mary Queen of Scots. Later, in the reign of Elizabeth I, Sir John, while still Sheriff of the County, had been imprisoned and fined for speaking against the Book of Common Prayer. By the time of the witches trial, in 1612, Mary's son James I was on the throne, and his vacillations between the protestant and catholic camps had served only to exacerbate religious passions. In this context, Jane Southworth, a member of a principal Catholic family, had decided to become a Protestant, and the Court concluded that the case against her was part of a family-inspired, Catholic strategy to disgrace her. In the end, Grace Sowerbutts did admit that she had been counselled by Christopher Southworth to fabricate the case against all three women.

Nine of the lower order Pendle witches and their accomplices were hanged, however, and surviving records of the testimony against them leaves a clear impression of a people in touch with the supernatural. Sorcery and spinning are, indeed, the very stuff of scary fairytale, and *Sleeping Beauty*, the story of a fairy uninvited to the christening of a king's daughter, who then spitefully curses the little girl, pronouncing that she will wound herself on a spindle and die (later converted to a sleep of a hundred years), is redolent of this period and was first published in the 17th century by the French raconteur, Charles Perrault.

Superstition was a theme throughout Britain at this time, but the Pendle Witches affair was highly visible and is interesting also because of the wide social range (from aristocrat to beggar) of the defendants. Soon there would be a different spirit alive in the land, one that would pull up by the roots the lives of many who lived in this ancient rural context. The 18th-century Age of Reason swept superstition aside and prepared the people of Lancashire for two centuries of invention, materialism and entrepreneurship, the like of which the world had never seen and could not have imagined.

But their sense of the supernatural was only ever driven underground, as perhaps was the craft of weaving a spell. In *The Road to Nab End,* William Woodruff recalls stories current when he was growing up in Blackburn in the 20th century of witches on Pendle Hill, elves in the roots of trees and under rocks, a white lady haunting of Samlesbury and ghostly horsemen across the moors. A belief in Fate remained especially strong – Jo herself is a strong believer in it to this day, and many of her novels evince this belief, explicitly in *A Time For Us* and *Jessica's Girl* – 'There's no use fighting it... These are the cards you've been dealt, Phoebe Mulligan. Play

The Great Hall, the oldest part of Samlesbury Hall, a few minutes drive north west of Blackburn, was built in 1325 by Gilbert de Southworth. Thomas, his great grandson, added the west wing, the oriel bay and the screen, and his son, John, was the lord whose strong Catholic beliefs had made him a supporter of Mary Queen of Scots and whose grandson had married Jane, one of the 'Samlesbury witches'.

In Whistledown Woman, *Samlesbury House is a 'Rest Home for Gentle Ladies' and the place where the 'foundling', Starlena, discovers that she has a mother. In* Outcast, *Breckleton House is positioned in the countryside of outer Breckleton, which we learn is only four miles from Blackburn by way of Preston New Road, which puts it in Samlesbury:*

'It was said that Breckleton House had been in the Crowther family for many generations... Immediately behind, the majestic trees formed a natural and fitting backdrop.' Outcast

them with the courage your mother gave you. And don't ever shame her.'

Commonly, still, people see omens in things, and in East Lancashire, Halloween attracts so many revellers to Pendle Hill that a police presence is required to keep traffic moving.

We should not, therefore, be so surprised to find a 'sense of the divine' among these 'dark Satanic Mills' as late as the 19th century, or to hear less far-distant echoes of the values of the rural hand-loom weaver as we pass through the hothouse of the industrial revolution into the 20th century.

Even as the Pendle witches walked to the gallows, weaving was becoming an ever more significant cottage industry. In 1635 it was reported that 'the poorer sort of people live by spinning and weaving linen cloths *all year long*, except in the time of harvest.' The industry was getting organised, encouraged by merchants and middle-men who worked as putter-outs, the 'putter-eawt' of Yates's poem, 'Owd Peter'.

The merchant would buy raw cotton and linen yarn from importers and sell it to the putter-out, who would sell it to the weaver. After manufacture, the selling process would be reversed, the putter-out purchasing the finished cloth from the weaver and selling it to the merchant, who would sell it on at market or export it.

Markets grew with this approach and, as the 17th century gave way to the 18th, the needs of domestic weavers began to influence the design of their cottages: long, low windows to maximise light on the ground floor, and, as we have seen, deep, damp cellars – fine cotton yarn being less likely to break in such conditions.

Industrial expansion did not, however, begin in earnest until after 1764, when inventors took the cotton industry by storm, speeding up first the spinning, then the weaving processes, before new transport systems to and from ports at Liverpool, London and eventually Manchester, speeded up the supply and distribution network.

These were exciting, innovative times and in *Outcast*, we get a picture of the more or less fully transformed scene in Blackburn in 1860, of the busy tempo, of the new middle-class lifestyle now supported by industry, of the factory set-up, which revolutionised the economy of the town, and of the less than satisfied workforce. Here, Caleb Crowther accompanies his niece, Emma Grady, to Wharf Mill, where she is about to 'learn the ropes' in the administrative office. The carriage takes them from Breckleton House, which we are told is just four miles from Blackburn by way of Preston New Road, through the middle class area of the town and on to Crowther's mill at Eanam.

We join them on Preston New Road:

At this early hour of eight a.m., there was much coming and going in every direction. The muffin-man was busy pushing his wicker-trolley along, his cloth cap perched

Preston New Road around the time of Emma Grady.

Thwaites and Dutton's were the big brewers in Blackburn, a town built on a tradition of cotton and ale. 'The brewery-wagon ambled along across the street, loaded with hefty wooden barrels brimful of draught beer.' Outcast

precariously over his forehead, his step a lively one, and his lips pursed together in the whistling of a jolly melody. The brewery-wagon ambled along across the street, loaded with hefty wooden barrels brimful of draught beer. As usual, the big black shires harnessed up front were magnificent in their polished brass and leather harness, with their long tails neatly plaited, and their manes gathered in rows of intricate decorated braids. So delighted was Emma by this scene, that she raised her hand in a friendly wave as the wagon rolled past them in the opposite direction.

'Mornin' to you,' called one of the two men from the drivers' bench, both of whom were dressed in dark coats and trim little bowlers, with light-coloured breeches tucked into their black knee-length boots. These boots were polished to such a deep mirror finish that they gave the impression of being shiny wet. Emma thought the whole ensemble to be a proud and dignified one – albeit for the purpose of carting ale!

As they passed the grander houses of Preston New Road, the ladies emerged in twos and threes. Some were dressed in flouncy crinoline style, while others favoured the newest bustle line; but all were bedecked in extravagant bonnets, and all were unquestionably elegant and resplendent. It amused Emma to see how her Uncle Caleb's countenance suddenly changed at the sight of all this female finery. At once, he was wearing the sickliest of smiles, and doffing his hat in exaggerated gentlemanly gestures – only to scowl and curse,

in characteristic fashion, when a four-horse carriage immediately behind began showing signs of impatience at his dawdling.

Emma grew more and more engrossed in the hustle and bustle as their route carried them farther away from the open countryside and wide roads, into the heart of industrial Blackburn town, with its narrow cobbled streets of tightly packed back-to-back houses, overlooked by towering and monstrous mill chimneys – themselves alive as they pumped out long creeping trails of choking black smoke.

On a day such as this – when the earth was parched and devoid of a breeze which might cool it or lift the billowing smoke higher into the air – the dark swirling clouds could only cling to the roofs and chimneys like a thick acrid blanket enveloping all beneath, and shutting out the brilliant sunlight from above. But, to the vast majority of Blackburn folk it was a natural and accepted thing which was as much a part of their daily lives as breathing itself. The cotton mills were the life-line of almost every man and his family, whether they were mill-workers, mill-owners, river-people, or others who benefited from this industry. They tolerated the smoke and the shrill scream of the mill whistle calling them from their beds at some ungodly hour, for cotton was the thread by which their very existence hung. It gave them work; it gave them a

'The Leeds to Liverpool Canal was a main artery from the Liverpool Docks to the various mills.'
Outcast

Above: *The canal at Cicely Bridge Mill, a short walk from Eanam Wharf, where Emma is headed.*

In Outcast, *Thadius Grady has two mills, one at Eanam Wharf (shown here) and the other on Cicely Top, where Jo's Mum worked.*

means by which they could raise their families in dignity; and, above all, it gave them a sense of pride and achievement.

Cotton mills were going up at an unprecedented rate all over Lancashire, but, here in Blackburn the programme of mill construction was staggering. Emma had inherited her papa's own pride in these great towering monstrosities, and she knew all their names – Bank Top Mill, Victoria Mill, Infirmary Mill – and, oh, so many more! Cotton was big business, keeping the town a hive of bustling activity. No hard-working mill-hand ever grew rich by it as his wages were too meagre; but, for the man with money to invest, the opportunities grew day by day. The Leeds to Liverpool Canal was a main artery from the Liverpool Docks to the various mills. Along this route the fuel and raw cotton which kept the mills alive was brought, thus affording a living to the many bargees who, with their families, dwelt in their colourful floating homes and spent most of their lives travelling to and from with their cargoes. This consisted mainly of raw cotton, unloaded from ships which carried it across the ocean from America.

Even Caleb Crowther's brooding mood, and her own feeling of bitterness towards him, couldn't quell Emma's enthusiasm as they clip-clopped towards the wharf. Oh, it brought back so many pleasant memories! Over Salford, along Railway Road, and into Eanam itself they went. Then, marked

Fleet of forty barges at Eanam Wharf, 1919. 'Along this route the fuel and raw cotton which kept the mills alive was brought, thus affording a living to the many bargees.' Outcast

by tall cylindrical chimneys reaching high into the sky, the mill came into sight. It was a huge building of some several storeys high, with each level lined with dozens upon dozens of long narrow windows. Soon, they were passing through the oppressive big iron gates of Wharf Mill.

As they came into view of the open warehouse doors, Emma could see a group of cloth-capped men gathered just inside, exchanging conversation – which was evidently causing a great deal of fist-waving, finger-wagging and head-shaking. It all seemed very intense. Suddenly, one of the men caught sight of Caleb Crowther approaching, whereupon there was a flurry of activity and the group dispersed immediately – all except for one hump-backed little fellow, who came towards them at an urgent pace.

'What the devil's going on here?' Caleb Crowther demanded as he brought the horse and vehicle to a halt. He clambered down as the hump-backed fellow caught hold of the horse's halter. 'Why aren't those men at their work, eh? . . . What the hell do they think I pay them wages for, eh? . . . eh?' His neck stretched forward and his voice grew shriller.

Later in the day, Emma's immediate manager suggests he take her on a tour of the mill:

Like Marlow and Sal Tanner, many bargees dwelt in their colourful floating homes and spent most of their lives travelling to and fro with their cargoes:

'First thing this morning, I cadged a ride on a barge that were going to Liverpool docks . . . I was sure there'd be some flowers coming in from one o' them far-off countries. But there weren't! At least, I never clapped eyes on 'em that's for sure. Then I hid in a wagon coming back, and it went all the way around Lancashire afore ending up in Blackburn.' Don't Cry Alone

Gregory Denton was so caught up in Emma's enthusiasm that he made a suggestion quite out of character. 'The ledgers can wait a while, Miss Grady,' he told her, 'and if you've a mind, I'd like to take you on a tour of the mill. . . so you can see for yourself what procedure is followed.'

Emma had already toyed with the idea of asking this very favour, once her clerical duties were done. 'Oh, I'd like that, Mr Denton,' she said, quickly climbing from the stool in case he should change his mind.

Just over an hour later, with only ten minutes to spare before midday, at which time Thomas was due to collect her, Emma followed Mr Denton down the stairs and into the warehouse. 'Thank you for taking me round,' she told him, greatly impressed by what she had seen. On visits with her papa, the farthest she'd been allowed to go was the office enclosure. But today she'd seen virtually the whole process the raw cotton had to go through. She had seen the loose bales thrown into a machine that tore any knots or lumps from the cotton; then she was taken to the cardroom where it was combed; after this she saw how the twisted rovings were spun on machines which were some twelve feet wide and two hundred feet long. The cotton was then washed, bleached, dried, beaten, folded and pressed, before being considered suitably finished and ready for use. In the loom-weaving shed, Emma had wondered how the mill-hands could stand the relentless noise, day after day, without going totally deaf.

They were now on the lowest level, where the bales of raw cotton, after being unloaded from the barges, were stored ceiling-high before samples were taken to ascertain the different grades and quality.

'Do you think you'll enjoy your work here, Miss Grady?' Denton ventured, feeling pleased with himself.

When Emma assured him that she'd had an exciting morning and was looking forward to learning all there was to know about the business, his face beamed with joy. 'Oh, that's grand!' he declared, feverishly nodding his head and rubbing his two hands together in a nervous fashion. 'That's right grand!'

By the look on his face as he leaned towards her, Emma could see he had a great deal more to say. But, at that moment there came a loud and frantic cry from the mouth of the warehouse, where the bales were brought in from the barges. This was immediately followed by a series of alarming noises and the unmistakable smell of fire.

Originally, in the domestic 'cardroom' stage of the pre-spinning stage, raw cotton was beaten clean and combed into parallel fibres between two hand-held, wired cards (like wire brushes). The spinner sat beside her spinning wheel and, on removing each batch of carded cotton from the teeth of a card, placed it to form a mass on one end of the spindle. The spindle was set up to be rotated by means of a drive band which encircled both it and the big hand wheel at the other end of the machine. The spinner would drive the hand wheel with one hand, and with the other she would gently pull a few fibres from the rotating cotton mass on the spindle. The rate of spin (which twisted the fibres as she pulled them out) and the speed at which she pulled them out, determined how many fibres made up the cross-section of yarn – how fine or coarse it was. Given that the cotton fibres massed on the end of the spindle were of different length, and that therefore their ends were drawn into the yarn at different and apparently, random moments, it is readily appreciated that the skill required to work the yarn by hand was considerable.

Weaving cloth is, in its simplest form, a matter of securing parallel lengths of yarn vertically into a structure (the warp) and then feeding more lengths crosswise (the weft) through them – the weft yarn going under and over each warp yarn successively. The weft yarn is contained in a shuttle, a bobbin-like device which leads it under and over the warp. To charge the shuttle with weft yarn, the weaver *kissed the shuttle* – drew the weft thread from the cop (a roll of thread wound on a spindle) by sucking it through a small hole at one end of the shuttle.

The series of inventions that triggered the industrial revolution in textiles worked on these processes. They included the flying shuttle, the spinning jenny, the water frame, the spinning mule, the steam engine and the power loom. The flying or fly-shuttle was invented in 1733 by John Kay. Previously, the weaver had to pass the shuttle through the warps by hand. For wide cloths more than one weaver had been required to pass it back and forth, but this new device ran on wheels and could be pulled rapidly across the

Hand loom incorporating the fly-shuttle invented by John Kay in 1733, first of the inventions that triggered the revolution.

Spinning jenny and cloth looms. Gradually the new machinery required more room. Warehouses began to be used for mass employment under one roof. The factory system thus began, with workers no longer owning their own wheels. Instead of working in their own homes at their own pace, spinners would now have to work in their employers' factories at the machines' pace.

loom with a cord. Then, in 1764, at Stanhill, James Hargreaves invented the spinning jenny. 'Jenny' means 'engine', and Hargreaves' jenny was the first handwheel-driven machine to spin more than one strand of yarn at once, it could spin eight spindles simultaneously.

By its very nature, Hargreaves' spinning jenny required a new stage of fibre preparation at the pre-spinning stage. The carded fibre was no longer massed onto the spindle, but made into a slender rope of parallel fibres (a 'roving') and wound around a bobbin. This is the point of the operation at which, more than 250 years later, Jo's mother became involved, albeit on a more sophisticated machine.

In 1769, Richard Arkwright's water frame was another multi-spindle spinning machine – so-called because, although designed to be driven by a horse, it came to be operated by a water wheel. Unlike Hargreaves' spinning jenny, however, which still worked on the principle of pulling fibres out of the carded cotton mass, the water frame operated on a principle invented by Lewis Paul some thirty years earlier, which drew the carded fibres out into yarn by passing them through pairs of rollers. The roving passed through the first pair – one roller lying on top of another – and on through a second pair, which, because it was operated at a faster speed, drew out (or drafted, as it is called) the fibres into the required yarn. It was a brilliant principle because it put less strain on the delicate fibres – they were less likely to break than on the spinning jenny – and it enabled continuous and faster operation. However, it wasn't as efficient at producing the *finest* yarn as the pulling-out principle, which continued in use, and it was only taken up in the 1780s by Samuel Crompton in his spinning mule, a kind of cross between Hargreaves' and Arkwright's inventions, capable of producing yarn sufficiently fine to be weaved into muslin.

This intense activity was attended by improvements to the preparatory and carding process, and of course to the final process, weaving, the most important of which was the power loom. But it was the new spinning machinery that first led to the factory system and began the move away from rural domestic production in Blackburn. The earliest mills in Blackburn, such as Wensley Fold Mill (1775), King Street Mill (1817) and Whalley Banks Mill (1818), were opened to house the new spinning machines. They represented a whole different way of working – workers no longer owned their own wheels; instead of working in their own homes at their own pace, spinners would now have to work in their employers' factories at the machines' pace.

Many were drawn in from outlying villages, as livelihoods were threatened by the factory operations. By 1800 there were 7,000 operatives in Blackburn, representing around 60% of the population. Twenty years later the number had more than doubled – a body of workers nearly 15,000 strong represented almost 70% of the town's burgeoning population.

The coming of the power loom greatly accelerated the shift from country to town. The Reverend Edmund Cartwright invented the first: 'Happening to be at Matlock in the summer of 1784,' he recorded, 'I fell in company with some gentlemen of Manchester, when the conversation turned on Arkwright's spinning machinery. One of the company observed that as soon as Arkwright's patent expired so many mills would be erected and so much cotton spun that *hands would never be found to weave it*. I replied that Arkwright must then set his wits to work to invent a weaving mill...'

Cartwright was given every reason why such an invention was impossible, but he countered with the news that someone had just invented a chess-playing automaton, and if that were possible then he was certain that he could invent a weaving mill. Cartwright was alluding to a recent demonstration in London of a figure apparently capable of playing chess. It turned out to be bogus, the chess-playing figure had been worked by a hidden hand, but the upshot was that Cartwright decided to have a crack at the power loom himself.

A year later his design was patented, but the machine was so slow and tiring to work that it could only be operated for short periods, which made it rather pointless. Nevertheless, Cartwright persisted and his second, improved loom was powered by a bull. Two years later he harnessed it (the loom that is) to a steam powered engine and managed to sell twenty-four machines to a Manchester firm. Alas, rioting hand-loom weavers burned the factory down.

Blighted as his project seems to have been, Cartwright's patents contained many of the elements used later for successful power looms, the first of which was patented by William Horrocks in 1802 and improved by Sharp & Roberts in 1822. From the 1820s, many new machine-making companies – Platt Brothers of Oldham, Hattersley & Sons of Keighley, and William Dickinson of Blackburn – were producing their own power-loom designs. Dickinson's Blackburn Loom was made at Harley Street Foundry in about 1840. A year later, William Kenworthy and James Bullough, also of Blackburn, patented various refinements,

Right: the Soho Foundry on Cicely Lane, the road leading over the bridge to Cicely mills. With the invention of the power loom, foundries began to spring up and from the 1820s they began to make and market their own machines.

which greatly improved its efficiency.

Power looms were first installed in Blackburn at Dandy Mill in 1825, from which time the writing was on the wall for hand-loomers. Derek Beattie charts the transition as follows. In 1780, the town's population was 5,000. In 1801, it amounted to 11,980, with 7,000 hand looms in use. In 1841 there were some 6,000 power looms in use and possibly as few as 1,000 hand looms. In 1907, when Blackburn was the cotton weaving capital of the world, there were around 130,000 people, no hand looms, but 79,403 power looms in use.

Aiding and abetting production improvements was a new transport system. In 1770, building work began on the Leeds-Liverpool canal. The canal, which would run commercial traffic until 1972, reached Blackburn in 1810, easing transportation not only of raw cotton and cloth, but of coal, lime and building materials mined in the neighbourhood – goods for powering the cotton industry and enabling the building programme that would be so closely bound up with it. Old warehouses were transformed into cotton mills, and space hitherto used in the bleaching industry was utilised for the huge domestic building programme.

The railway was the next fillip, the Preston-Blackburn line opening in 1846. However, it was never the dominant force that the canal turned out to be, as Mike Clarke notes in Alan Duckworth's

The new inventions in the cotton industry increased the speed of production and made it more economical. The improved transport enhanced supply of raw cotton and distribution of finished cloth. Blackburn Railway Station – 'There it was, a grand building with iron structures and huge arches at the entrance.'
Looking Back

Aspects of Blackburn. In 1851 the canal's cargo business was leased to a group of local railway companies, including the Lancashire and Yorkshire Railway, which gave it a virtual monopoly on transport in East Lancashire. Mill owners, increasingly ill-served by this monopoly, pressured the canal company to revoke the lease. By 1880 the Lancashire and Yorkshire Railway was laying off staff at Burnley because the canal had taken over much of their traffic. As a result new boat yards sprang up and business boomed in those that were already servicing the canal.

Outcast, the novel that introduces Emma Grady and Sal Tanner, both of whom we have already met, makes use of Jo's knowledge of the canal, picked up firsthand in her youth. Marlow Tanner, Sal's brother, with whom Emma falls in love, lives with Sal on a barge, ferrying cargoes of coal and cotton up and down the Leeds and Liverpool waterways. Here, Emma steps for the first time into the depths of the Tanner barge and gets a surprise:

'"What's it like? Oh, it's grand, Molly lass . . . right grand! There's no better life in this 'ere world, than rovin' the waterways in yer own barge . . . wi' yer own pots an' pans an' the treasures about yer."' Alley Urchin

It was the first time Emma had ever been inside a barge, and it had been a great surprise. Not for a moment had she expected to see such a cosy and exceptionally pretty home as this. All the walls and ceiling were made of highly-polished panels. In the living-quarters the walls were decorated with lovely brass artefacts – plates, old bellows and the like; from the ceiling hung three oil-lamps of brass and wood, each sparkling and meticulously kept; there were two tiny dressers, both made of walnut and displaying small china ornaments – which, according to Sal, were 'put away when we're on the move'; as were the china plates which were propped up on shelves beneath each porthole; the horse-hair chairs were free-standing, but the dressers were securely fixed to the floorboards. There was also a small cast-iron fire, and the narrow

'It was the first time Emma had ever been inside a barge. Not for a moment had she expected to see such a cosy and pretty home as this.' Outcast

galley which was well-stocked and spotless. In one of the two bedrooms there was a tiny dresser with a tall cupboard beside it, and a deep narrow bunk beneath a porthole. Emma had been astonished that everything a person might need could be provided in such a limited space.

Later, in *Vagabonds*, Marlow builds up a canal cargo business – Tanner's Transporters, part of the new boat yard boom:

He had worked his way up from being a bargee who struggled for a living, going cap-in-hand to such men as Caleb Crowther who once owned most of the mills along the wharf – property that, by rights, had belonged to Emma... Marlow Tanner may not look as smooth and smarmy as the next gent...but he's a better gent than ever you're likely to find. A proper credit to the blokes who work for him. There ain't one of us who wouldn't stretch ourselves to the limit if he were to ask. Teks god care of us he do...through thick and thin. You'll never find a better gaffer than Marlow Tanner.

The new inventions in the cotton industry increased the speed of production and made it more economical. The improved transport enhanced supply of raw cotton and distribution of finished cloth. Yet, for some considerable time, the new machines couldn't manage the same high quality of production, the fine workmanship, which the

By 1880 the Lancashire and Yorkshire Railway was laying off staff at Burnley because the canal had taken over much of their traffic. As a result new boat yards sprang up and business boomed in those that were already servicing the canal.

supreme practitioners among hand-loom weavers achieved. At Mellor, on the north-western fringe of Blackburn, for example, there was a tradition of extraordinary skills in the hand spinning and weaving of cloth. Indeed, such was the quality of craftsmanship in patterned cloth that hand weaving would remain an important industry in Mellor for nearly half a century after the introduction of the power loom.

Nevertheless, the sheer speed of production of the new machines would win out, and in time even the finest cotton producers in China and India were unable to compete. In 1913 Lancashire as a whole could boast exports of seven billion yards of cloth.

In Blackburn, resistance to the hijacking of the traditional domestic industry began early. The first mill to take on a spinning jenny had been Peel's Mill. In 1768 rioters ran amok, attacking both the mill and inventor James Hargreaves' cottage. The mill belonged to the family of Sir Robert Peel, British Prime Minister 1834-5 and 1841-6, founder of the Metropolitan Police and instrumental in the repeal of the restrictive Corn Laws. He was born in Fish Lane, Blackburn, twenty years after the attack, but the family was eventually driven out by worker riots.

The revolution was dramatic. The cottage spinners and weavers were not about to give up their freedom without a fight and their passions were whipped up by putter-outs, who would of course lose their livelihoods in the new factory system. Worse, the new mill owners instigated a deliberate policy of cleansing the countryside of the old tradition.

A common view in the history books is that enclosures and new agricultural methods were displacing the rural people anyway. But a government enquiry in 1838 reveals a mill-owner strategy of rural de-population, of coercion and oppression, of herding agricultural workers, hand spinners and weavers from their cottages in outlying villages into the new mill-worker colonies in Blackburn, of mill owners buying up hand weavers' cottages, evicting their tenants and then offering them salvation in the form of jobs at their Blackburn mills. It is small wonder that the weavers turned nasty.

In his autobiography, William Woodruff describes the legal backlash – how workers who had burned factories down were transported to Australia and paid with their lives. In 1812 in West-Houghton they hanged three men, and a boy of fourteen went to the gallows calling for his mother. In the 1820s in Blackburn, thousands of workers, armed with pikes, hammers and cro-bars smashed every power loom they could lay their hands on.

April 1826 saw the last riot. It came just a year after power looms had been installed in Dandy Mill, and at a serious downturn in the industry which saw more than half the population of Blackburn on poor relief.

Six thousand rioters participated. The Bay Horse Hotel, in the Church Street/Salford Bridge area, was occupied and drunk dry, and more than 200 power looms were wrecked. One John Hartley was among the rioters arrested by the High Constable's men. His family had been in cotton for 100 years, since Thomas Hartley, 'a poor boy of Blackburn', was apprenticed as a weaver in 1730. Many of those arrested were committed for trial at the Quarter Sessions, though not Hartley himself, whose family would remain in the industry until 1991.

Reading such a statistic underlines the reality of the *living continuity* of the tradition, and recommends the historical approach in attempting to understand what it was that made the Blackburn community tick at any period, at least up to the mid-20th century when Jo was soaking it all in. This is, of course, Jo's own approach; the story settings of her novels range from 1850 (*Tomorrow The World*) to 1985 (*A Time For Us*).

The hand-loomers failed to stop the revolution, but, as Beattie points out, they probably did delay the mechanisation of the industry. By 1835 Blackburn was accountable for barely 5% of the power looms in use in the county.

Once the factory system got going, however, the character of the Blackburn spinners and weavers would be challenged by harsh discipline, by regular depressions in the industry, by general poverty and the often appalling conditions in which they had to live and work. The town would become a centre of manufacture for the world, but it would also become a cesspit of human misery.

What the cotton workers went through deeply affected and hardened their character, fusing them into a community. Certain values

In 1830, the working day averaged thirteen hours (6 a.m. to 7 p.m.), with forty minutes break for lunch. This might seem better than the 16-hour day worked by the traditional hand-loom weaver at home, but the factory operative earned only as much as an unskilled builder's labourer, and it had been better to be poor in the country, where you could at least grow your own food and enjoy less obnoxious living and working conditions.

rose up within the community to become its characteristic expression: a survivor-sense of self-worth, a resolution born of never getting something for nothing, a work ethic born of want and driven by what Woodruff describes as 'tight-lipped, dogged pride,' which led some, as we shall see, into all kinds of problems. Work became, as Chris Aspen notes in *The Cotton Industry*, 'a virtue to be cultivated,' and less doughty men abroad became worried lest the trait be catching. In 1844, Frenchman Leon Faucher wrote:

19th-century weaving shed. In 1844, Frenchman Leon Faucher wrote: 'Overwork is a disease which Lancashire has inflicted upon England and which England in turn has inflicted upon Europe.'

'Overwork is a disease which Lancashire has inflicted upon England and which England in turn has inflicted upon Europe.' All this in the face of often terrible working conditions in the mills.

Besides the noise, there were some extraordinary environmental problems, such as the pumping of unclean water as steam into the factories in order to create an atmosphere favourable to the production of fine cotton yarn. Not only did this tainted steam produce an unhealthily polluted atmosphere in which to work, but the contrast with the atmosphere outside encouraged further infection and disease.

In 1830, the working day averaged thirteen hours (6 a.m. to 7 p.m.), with forty minutes break for lunch. This might seem better than the 16-hour day frequently worked by the traditional hand-loom weaver, but the factory operative earned only as much as an unskilled builder's labourer, and while, in times of depression, the rural hand-loom weaver might fail to earn enough to feed his family, it had been better to be poor in the country, where you could at least grow your own food and enjoy less obnoxious living and working conditions.

The wage problem in the cotton industry had to do with hand workers being traditionally ill-paid and the fact that much of the work could be done by women, who, it was accepted, could be paid less than men. The new mill owners saw no reason to change this state of affairs. Among factory operatives in the early 1900s, females outnumbered males by two to one, and 44% of all married women in the town worked. A cotton-mill family might find consolation in the

Unusually, here was an industry that offered work for women as well as men, but this fact helped fix the wages artificially low – it was taken for granted that women could be paid little. So, while female as well as male family members could find work in the industry, the wages were so poor that it took two to feed a family and if there came a time when only one member of that family was fit or able to work, he or she might not be able to earn enough to make ends meet.

The emancipation of women in the workplace, prevalent in the cotton industry, did not spill over into the home, where domestic work began for women as soon as the factory shift was over.

fact that female as well as male members could find work in the industry, but so poor were the wages that it took two to feed a family and if, for whatever reason, there came a time when not more than one member of that family was fit or able to work, he or she would not

There were repeated outbreaks of cholera and typhus in the town owing to untreated sewage. The Blakewater (seen above, today) *was described as an elongated cesspool, 'spreading the seeds of disease and death and even contaminating the very food of the living.'*

be able to earn enough to make ends meet.

While the machines of industry grew, the machinery to run this new society, lagged far behind. We read of 'heaps of refuse, debris and offal', of hopeless drainage, of standing pools and a terrible stench.

In June, 1849, Charles Tiplady wrote a letter bewailing the pollution that industry had brought to the Blakewater. Tiplady is interesting. Between 1839 and his death in 1873 he kept a diary, extracts from which had been transcribed in the 19th century by a man called Abram, who had been working on a history of Blackburn. The diary, a fascinating record of this significant period, had then mysteriously disappeared and was only recently rediscovered – retrieved from a dustbin by Nottingham auctioneers Mellors & Kirk during a house clearance. As I write, it is being transcribed by the Blackburn Local History Society, who, with the Victoria & Albert Museum in London, Blackburn Library and the Museum & Art Gallery secured the diary for the town. Tiplady's shop (as already said, he was a printer and bookseller) was in Church Street, near Salford Bridge. Like Jo's in nearby Henry Street, the cellar regularly flooded when the Blakewater was high. A contemporary report on sanitary conditions in the town gives us an inkling as to what such a flooding brought into the building. The Blakewater is described as an elongated cesspool, 'spreading the seeds of disease and death and even contaminating the very food of the living.'

There were indeed repeated outbreaks of cholera and typhus in the town owing to untreated sewage. In 1856 work began on a proper sewage system, but if you lived in a canal-side area, you were still three times more likely to die early than in sweeter smelling Preston New Road, where the toffs hung out. In 1858, the Blackburn Infirmary was founded by a high profile mill-owning family by name of Pilkington. It figures in *Angels Cry Sometimes*, where Grandma Fletcher's clogs echo on the stone flag floors and she tells Marcia, her daughter, 'I never 'ave liked the smell o' these places.' It also figures in *Looking Back* and in *Her Father's Sins*, where Queenie gives her view of the hospital in the 1950s –

> A scarred relic of a grand Victorian era. In its heyday, people from all walks of life would marvel at its square strength and ornate façade; suitably impressed also at the wonderful facilities provided by its costly construction and choice personnel. Now, however, with the fading of its youthful bloom beneath the relentless ravages of time, the building no longer drew a profusion of praise, but a torrent of complaint and abuse. The dampness breathed in the walls, and the wind persistently whistled through the ill-fitting window-jambs. The long snaking corridors, devoid of windows, were dark and dungeon-like. Their shadowy unclean appearance ensured that no one ever lingered in their recesses.

Besides damp and infested conditions and poverty, poor diet also

took its toll, especially on infants, more than half of whom died before their fifth birthday, just a year before they could be engaged in work. In the Lancashire coal industry in the early 1840s, boys would begin working at between 6 and 11 years of age. In *Don't Cry Alone*, which opens in 1868, Maisie's son, Matthew, works down the mines; he's only 11. The younger boys were no good for heavy work and occupied positions such as door-tender. They would crouch miles underground for twelve hours a day in total darkness, until occasionally a wagon came along and the air-door had to be opened. One inspector noted that these boys were particularly shy, which is scarcely surprising... 'Exertion there is none, nor labour, further than is requisite to open and shut a door. As these little fellows are always the youngest in the pits, I have generally found them very

Church Street in the 19th century when Charles Tiplady had his shop here. Tiplady's diary, a fascinating record of this significant period, was only recently rediscovered – retrieved from a dustbin by Nottingham auctioneers Mellors & Kirk during a house clearance.

The Blackburn Infirmary today, no longer the damp, dark and dungeon-like edifice of the 1950s.

'The anaesthetic stench of the Infirmary enveloped them as Marcia pushed open the heavy inner doors. Everywhere there was a sense of urgency, as busy white-coated doctors and 'slips-o-lasses', as Grandma Fletcher insisted on calling them, hurried back and forth, intent only on the task in hand. Grandma Fletcher's clogs echoed on the stone flag floors as she and Marcia hurried down the corridors. 'I never 'ave liked the smell o' these places,' she told Marcia in a loud whisper, as she scurried to keep up with her daughter. Angels Cry Sometimes

shy.' Less lonely a job was that of gigger, who looked after the load balance on a wagon of coal. Giggers were also among the youngest of the child workers down the mine.

These past weeks Maisie had been concerned about the boy. He seemed to be unusually quiet; although of course he had never been the lively little chatterbox that Cissie was. All the same, Maisie had noticed how withdrawn he'd become of late, and how he was always wanting to go to bed afore time. Lately, too, he had not been eating enough to keep a sparrow alive. She looked at him now, with his floppy mass of brown hair and eyes as violet as her own, and she though how tender he was at eleven years old to be working alongside grown men down the mines. Not for the first time, she asked herself whether there could have been any other way she might have organised things. But the answer was always the same, When her darling man was lost in those same bloody mines, she had done the best she could; although there was never a day went by when she didn't regret the way young Matthew seemed to be paying the biggest price of all. 'Your dad would have been so proud of you, lad,' she said now in a choking voice...

In spinning and weaving, children had always helped as fetchers and carriers, as well as in the least skilled and less labour-intensive tasks. As mechanisation increased the speed and efficiency of the industry, children could take a greater part in the process. Moreover, in the cost-conscious factory system, child workers were popular because they were cheap and available. The jobs they did were often menial, such as 'scavenging', namely crawling into small and sometimes dangerous places in the machinery which would be hard to clean out otherwise, but might involve the kind of skill that would enable the child to avoid personal injury, as in replacing the metal combs in the automated carding process – 'a hand inserted too far into the machine could result in loss of finger tips,' as Michael Winstanley writes in his excellent book, *Working Children in Nineteenth-Century Lancashire*.

Often there would be little genuine effort to bring a child on and into the more skilled areas of the industry. When a boy-apprentice became a man, he might well be laid off in favour of a younger, cheaper worker. Apprentices often worked for food and lodging and sleep in a room in the mill or in a separate house. Commonly it was the poorest and orphan children who suffered most from the system. A cotton apprenticeship was a way of *disposing* of the 'problem' of their very existence. As young as six a lad might work twelve to fifteen-hour shifts, which dovetailed into one another so that one clocking off would steal into the warm bed of another clocking on.

Conditions and standards of care created misery of Dickensian proportions. Said a mill worker in 1831, when asked how the mill masters kept the children to their work during these long, intensive hours, day after day: 'Sometimes they would tap

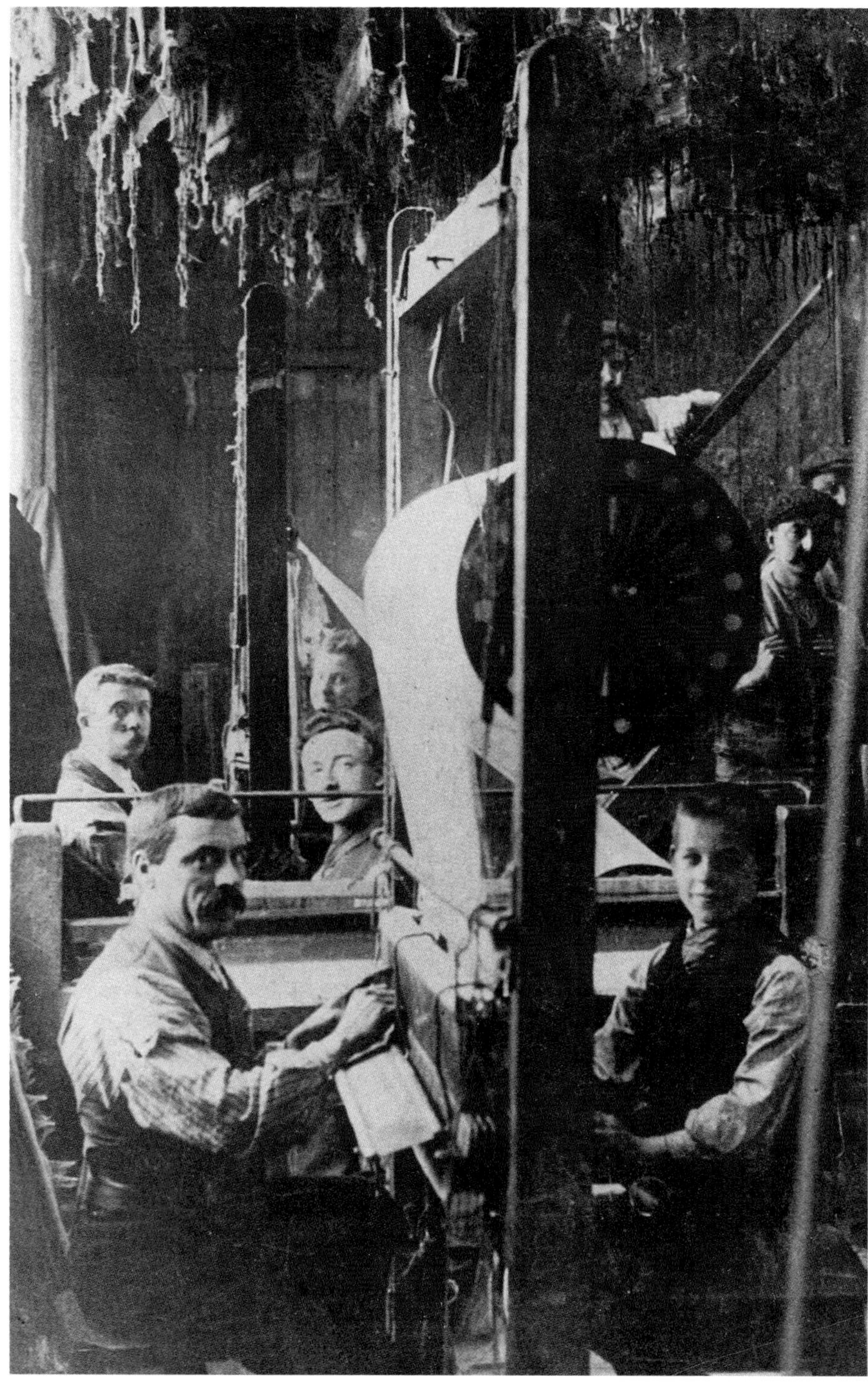

In spinning and weaving, children had always helped as fetchers and carriers, as well as in the least skilled and less labour-intensive tasks. As mechanisation increased the speed and efficiency of the industry, children could take a greater part in the process. Moreover, in the cost-conscious factory system, child workers were popular because they were cheap and available... so long as they made it past their fifth birthday, which half of them did.

them over the head, or nip them on the nose, or give them a pinch of snuff, or throw water in their faces...or shake them about to keep them waking.'

In a factory environment output was the only priority, every-

The jobs children did were often menial, such as sweeping the factory floor and 'scavenging', namely crawling into small and sometimes dangerous places in the machinery which would be hard to clean out otherwise – 'a hand inserted too far into the machine could result in loss of finger tips,' as Michael Winstanley notes.

thing and everyone yielded to that principle, and discipline could be fierce, as one 12-year-old boy put on record in 1832: 'One time I was struck by the master on the head with his clenched fist, and kicked when I was down. I saw one girl trailed by the hair of her head, and kicked by him...until she roared, "Murder!" several times. There was one orphan girl who spun at the same frame with me... She was engaged at the mill for three years, for food and clothes. She one day got entangled in the machinery till all her clothes were torn off her back. When she was taken out, she was very much abused [by the overlooker] for letting herself get caught up.'

A contemporary report conceded that there was a serious health risk: 'These children are usually too long confined to work in close rooms, often during the night; the air they breathe from the oil, etc, employed in the machinery and other circumstances is injurious;

Boys at work in the carding room. Often there would be little effort to bring a child on and into the more skilled areas of the industry. When a boy-apprentice became a man, he might well be laid off in favour of a younger, cheaper worker. Apprentices often worked for food and lodging, and slept in a room in the mill. As young as six lads might work twelve to fifteen-hour shifts, which dovetailed into one another so that one lad clocking off would steal into the warm bed of another clocking on.

little regard is paid to their cleanliness, and frequent changes from a warm and dense to a cold and thin atmosphere, are predisposing causes to sickness and disability...and has debilitated the constitution and retarded the growth of many.'

The first Factory Act (1819) prohibited employment of children under nine years of age. The Act instituted a maximum twelve-hour working day (excluding meal breaks) for children under 16, but enforcement was left to local JPs and was lax. Other Acts followed in 1833, 1844 and 1867, but in 1851, and still in 1871, more than 40% of all children between 10 and 14 years of age, living in Lancashire, worked, and in 1871 the county accounted for one sixth of the nation's working boys between these ages, and nearly a quarter (22%) of all working girls in the age group. In Blackburn, as late as 1911, over 90% of all 14-year-olds were in employment, and 84% of all girls of that age. Further Acts raised the legal minimum working age of children to 12 years in 1901, 14 in 1920 and 16 in 1937.

This did not stop Jo leaving school and working in a vinegar bottling factory from the age of 14, and she remembers just how fast the experience removed her childhood innocence: 'Just before leaving Blackburn I worked in a vinegar bottling factory. There was a carrousel, one woman would put the empty vinegar

The old Blackburn Grammar School in Freckleton Street, the other side of King Street from where Jo attended St Anne's School.

Founded in 1514, the Grammar School was joined in 1763 by the Girls Charity School, and in the following century, the Dame schools, also private.

The subsequent mill-backed Church schools, which started out as Sunday Schools, and, in the 1870s, a handful of State schools uniformly managed to ensure that few would escape the mill floor as their early destination. Records for literacy and attendance were abysmal.

bottles in, the next woman would fill them with vinegar, then one would put the tops on, I would put the labels on and someone would take them out and crate them up and someone else would come and take the crates away. Now that place was at the foot of the road where Cicely Bridge Mill was, near the bridge. It ran down to the river, and it had these big heavy green doors, like rubber doors, you know to run the trolleys through and out to the lorries, and the rats would come up from the river and you could be sitting doing your job with the rats running about your feet. That was my first job, and I was only there for about a month before mum and dad split up. But the things that I learnt from those women around that carrousel. My god! I was inducted into life very quickly. A lot of that has gone into my books, things I heard, things I heard them telling each other.'

The Act of 1844 is interesting because it actually reduced the minimum working age from nine to eight in the mills, but insisted that 8 to 13-year-olds could only work if they also attended school – six and a half hours per day in the mills plus three hours per day (Monday to Friday only!) at school. The mill masters were allowed to dock 2d per day from a child's wages towards the cost of schooling!

'The half-time system', as it became known, was actually the first compulsory schooling anywhere in the country, and in the context of the town's severe truancy problem the idea was touted as progressive, when in fact, it cleverly ensured the continuance of child labour in the face of growing opposition.

'No school, no mill; no mill, no money,' was the child workers' chant, and it was the mill's gain, not the children's.

The Education Acts of 1870 and 1876 gave School Boards and School Attendance Committees the authority to make schooling compulsory to 10 years of age, but half-timers escaped it. Blackburn had as many as 6,000 children in the half-time system even as late as 1875. Then, from effect in 1876, the 1874 Factory Act made it illegal for any child to be a half-timer until he or she was 10. Thereafter, further Acts nudged the full-time school leaving age up to 11 years in 1893, 12 in 1900, 14 in 1918. However, in 1909, in three schools monitored in Blackburn there were still 208 half-timers out of 286 children in the 12 to 14 age group.

Even after these Education Acts, children in the state sector would receive only a very basic education in the 3Rs to prepare them for the mills. The mills were the focus. However bright you turned out, as one worker put it, 'them days we *had* to go to the mill. You weren't asked.' When, in 1870, the Blackburn School Board, dominated by mill owners, was encouraged by the Education Act to utilise ratepayers' money to start up state schools, it only ever opened four, happy to leave the business to the Church schools. Together, the 19th-century record of State and Church in the matter of literacy was abysmal, with the poorest the really hopeless cases. Many would go on to undertake the most lowly jobs in society, many were Irish, but many also would become what Beattie refers to as 'men on the tramp'.

'He obviously comes from the sort of background where it's more profitable to learn the art of pick-pocketing than to know how to write his own name.'
A Little Badness

In 1862 there were 3,387 vagrants provided for in the Blackburn Union Workhouse on Haslingden Road, now Queen's Park Hospital. Jo's novel *Cradle of Thorns* gives us the area with a touch of childhood nostalgia and a nod to the nearby Robin Hood pub, still a favourite today. But *Miss You Forever,* which spans the years 1855-1912, gives a picture of the reality of life as a vagrant. The novel sets out in the company of Kathleen Peterson, a tramp who keeps her whole life in an old tapestry bag. There are other than trampish qualities lurking behind Kathleen's unkempt appearance, as it happens, but the portrait is true enough:

> The old woman had lost count of the times when she'd been jeered at, spat at, laughed at, or chased away at the sharp end of a pitchfork. People were wary of newcomers, especially "newcomers" with no fixed abode or means of earning a living... In her lonely treks Kathleen Peterson had travelled the length and breadth of Britain. She had tramped across the green fields of the Emerald isle and climbed the hills of Scotland. She had stayed in the Welsh valleys, travelled every nook and cranny of England, but her heart always brought her back to Blackburn.

Kathleen was always accompanied by 'a mangy old dog she had found snuggling up to her when she awoke in an alley one cold February morning. He was a dolly mixture of black and brown, with a long, meandering splash of white down his nose, and a speckle of

Blackburn Union Workhouse, now Queen's Park Hospital, on Haslingden Road, a road that was like a second home to Nell Reece in Cradle of Thorns*: 'Long and staggered, with cobbled ground, it was packed on either side with pretty terraced houses. There was a grocery shop, a big piece of waste ground where the children played, and a lively, popular pub called the Robin Hood* (above) *where, on Friday and Saturday nights, the working men would congregate and put the world to rights, Molly's Joe being the first to arrive and the last to leave.'*

grey round his whiskers... He reminded Kathleen of an old man she had known as a child... His name was Mr Potts. "What else can I call you?" she had asked the dog, and so he was given the old man's name.' Later Kathleen is badly beaten up by thugs and Mr Potts killed.

The poverty of education in the town, together with the high incidence of both parents working, led to the grand tradition of truancy, to which I have alluded. In 1871 only three-quarters of children on the registers of publicly inspected schools turned up daily. Here, in an excerpt from *Don't Cry Alone*, a novel set at the point that the Education Act came into force, Cissie, the little flower-seller, is playing truant in the market and doing her best to avoid detection:

The man from the School Board had been wandering the market-place earlier, looking for children to march off to school. Always on the look-out for him, Cissie had managed to hide until he'd gone; but even now he might be hanging about, she thought, nervously glancing from side to side. 'Let's be off,' she said with a mischievous grin. Then, whistling through her teeth, she took up step beside Beth and the two of them headed away from the market, down Cort Street and on to Ainsworth Street, with Cissie excitedly chattering and Beth quietly listening, thinking what a delightful little creature her companion was.

Later, Cissie's mother, Maisie, persuades her daughter to take advantage of the new system afforded by the Education Act, but the girl's feelings about school are Jo's as a child:

'I hate it!' Cissie toyed with her food. Somehow her appetite had altogether gone and her mood was defiant as she stared up at Maisie. 'You wouldn't like it, would you, Mam?' she cried. 'Nobody in their right mind would like it. You

Fruit stalls on Blackburn Market in Cissie Armstrong's time. Jo shared Cissie's view of education, and she would dodge the truant officer as successfully as did Cissie 100 years earlier in the market-place.

don't know how awful it is, or you wouldn't make me go there. Honest to God, Mam, it's just like a prison! That's what it is, Mam . . . it's worse.'

'Give over, our Cissie,' Maisie told her impatiently. 'How in God's name can it be worse than a prison?' She was rapidly losing her temper. 'Yer ain't shackled to the wall, are yer?'

'No, but we might as well be,' retorted Cissie.

'Yer ain't! And that's enough,' warned Maisie. 'And yer ain't fed on bread and water, are yer?'

'We ain't fed on nothing, that's what.'

'And yer ain't made to wear them overalls with arrows on, are yer?' Maisie persisted.

Hard times began in earnest in 1862, and starvation threatened even the street urchins' games. 'They'd swapped hoops and marbles and traded daydreams, they'd laughed and fought together.'
Jessica's Girl

'Well . . . no,' Cissie reluctantly conceded, realising with disgust and a sinking heart that she was losing the argument. 'But sometimes Mr Siniter flogs the boys with the cat-o'-nine-tails!' she added hopefully.

'And no doubt the buggers deserve it,' retorted Maisie, being wise to Cissie's ploy; although she didn't doubt for one minute that the boys were flogged, some of the lasses too she wouldn't be surprised.

'Oh, Mam!' Cissie rounded the table and tugged at Maisie's apron. 'I hate being squashed in amongst ninety brats, and having my knuckles rapped when I don't understand what Mr Siniter's telling me. I don't understand sums, and all them strange words. Don't make me go. Please, Mam.'

'Yer have to go, lass,' Maisie argued. 'That there Gladstone fella made it legal that all childer have to attend school 'til they're ten year old. If that education bloke finds I've failed in me duty, like as not the bugger'll have me clapped in irons!'

A cyclical habit of depression and relative prosperity – an uncertain, see-saw of work, piece-work and being out of work – characterised the cotton industry from the word go and made workers alternately bitter and thankful that a day's work was in prospect, as Jo notes in *Angels Cry Sometimes*:

Blackburn was a textile town, and the folks here, as in many other Lancashire towns, earned their bread and butter in gaunt formidable buildings from the Victorian era, whose grim outlines were ever silhouetted against the sky like so many sentries watching over the towns below. Folks were more than thankful for the work these great mills brought them, because the depression had struck particularly hard in the North of England, with many a man denied the dignity of work. And many a family going hungry! There was deep bitterness in the ranks, with high-running emotions against the Government, who, many claimed, had turned its back on the working class.

The workers had little choice. There were few alternatives to work in a mill. The Thwaites family brewery (the name pronounced in Blackburn without the 'h') had been founded in 1797, Dutton's was another of the town's brewers, and a few other industries did spring up, such as construction and engineering, but these were dependent on the cotton industry: building houses for mill workers, mills, looms, steam engines. The economy of the town turned on cotton. Cotton dominated everything, and when cotton failed, as periodically it did, then everyone suffered. The worst period of depression, from 1862, really ate into the heart of the town. Jim Heyes records in *Aspects of Blackburn* that '30,000 of a population of 62,126 were receiving relief.' The figure probably underestimates the suffering, for, as Tiplady noted at the time, 'Pride made many refuse relief.'

A year earlier, in 1861, civil war had broken out in North

America, and a blockade of the Confederate ports (the southern states, whence Blackburn's raw cotton came) prevented exports, leading to 'bad times, mass unemployment and famine' in Blackburn, even starvation.

Before the war broke out, Blackburn's mills had been overstocked with raw fibre, and mill owners were keen to play down the risk, some feeling that articles appearing in the *Blackburn Standard* were already unsettling the workforce. Many were clearly jittery. Tiplady noted in his diary on February 15, 1861, that these were 'troublous times...a majority of hands suspended work' in the mills over a disagreement about wages.

In *Outcast*, Caleb Crowther is one of those mill owners keen to dampen speculation:

The Thwaites family brewery had been founded in 1797 at Salford – at that time the Blakewater was the secret ingredient of its beer – and a few other industries did spring up, such as construction and engineering, but all were dependent in one way or another on the cotton industry: building houses for mill workers, mills, looms, steam engines. The economy of the town turned on cotton. Cotton dominated everything. When cotton failed everyone suffered.

Suddenly the lucrative factory system was terminally threatened. The American Civil War (1861-1865) caused Blackburn its worst Depression, but industry did survive.

'There's a war brewing in America, I tell you!' The portly fellow tipped the brandy glass to his lips and drained it dry. Then, taking a chunky cigar from his top pocket, he placed it between his teeth and began biting on it. 'It won't be long now before Lincoln's elected to office, and, with the Republicans so intent on this anti-slavery policy, there'll be fur flying in no time. You mark my words, there'll be war on the other side of the Atlantic!'

'I hope to God you're wrong, Harrison!' declared a small, square-looking fellow seated in the deep, leather armchair by the fire, his weasel-features bathed by the heat from the flames, and his eyes most anxious as they swept the eight figures seated around the room. 'Each of us here has all our money sunk in the Lancashire cotton industry. Should there be a war in America . . . and the issue is the slaves who pick the cotton which runs our mills . . . it could mean catastrophe for Lancashire. And for every one of us here!' The thought appeared to horrify him because he was suddenly on his feet and pacing anxiously up and down.

'You're exaggerating!' protested one man.

'It's a fact though,' said another, 'it was May when Lincoln was nominated for the presidency – six months ago! And just look how the southern states have put up every obstacle to keep him from coming to office. There is strong feeling. There bloody well is! If you ask me, it's a situation which needs to be watched most carefully!'

'You're panicking, the lot of you!' intervened a bald-headed man. 'I'm telling you, there'll be no war. The cotton will be shipped in just as regularly as it's ever been and the mills of Lancashire will continue to thrive, just as they are now.' With that said, he leaned back in his chair, embracing one and all with a smug expression.

'Gentlemen.' All eyes turned to look at Caleb Crowther. So far, he had made no contribution to the debate which, since the men's departure from the dinner table to the sanctuary of the library, had become somewhat heated. Now, however, he strode to the centre of the room where he tactfully waited to ensure that he held their absolute attention. When satisfied, he continued in a sombre tone, 'The very reason you were all invited here tonight, was to discuss this matter. Of late, there has been too much talk of what's happening in America and it's time to put an end to it!' Here his vivid eyes pausing, he oppressively scrutinized each of his guests in turn, and each was visibly affected. 'Isn't it enough that the *Blackburn Standard* puts out such articles that have our very mill-hands stopping their work to air their views and spread even more unrest? It's up to us . . . the owners . . . to set an example! If we show ourselves to be affected by unfounded gossip and troublesome rumours, then how the devil are we to expect any different from the fools we employ?' Though his expression was one of fury, his voice was remarkably calm. 'I say there will be no war in America. The slaves will pick the cotton as they always have, and the people of Lancashire will go on processing it in our mills. There is no place here for scaremongers!'

There had been need of a soup kitchen before, in the 1840s, and in 1826 and again in 1847 a visitor system had had to be organised to rescue the truly starving, too proud to claim relief – public officers going round to houses, as in the photograph above, winkling out the worst cases.

Soon, however, the American Civil War and its implications for Blackburn were apparent. Mills began short-term working, some factories closed, and somehow, as Tiplady recorded, even the weather conspired to depress. November 16, 1861: 'First fall of snow this Winter – heavy, followed by a keen frost – time fairly gloomy; work scarce; cotton dear; money bad to get.'

The town set up a Central Relief Committee and on January 20, 1862, Tiplady wrote: 'Great distress in consequence of the American War. A soup kitchen established in the Town.'

The soup kitchen was in fact on Cleaver Street, where '2,400 quarts of soup were dispensed each day; meal and bread on alternate days.' On March 5, he noted, 'Heavy fall of snow. The distress of the Operatives continues; and relief is afforded to thousands of unemployed poor.'

In *Outcast*, bargee Marlow Tanner tells her sister, Sal, of the indignity of the very needy:

'I don't need to tell you, Sal...you know well enough. You've seen them . . . in the soup queues. And you've seen the boarded-up houses where folks have been thrown out because they can't pay the rent. We at least have some work, and we have a roof over our heads.'

'The onset of poverty, real degrading poverty, had crept up on them, in the guise of false hopes. Now optimism was a luxury; yet Queenie could not be daunted. While she had Aunt Biddy the world was bearable, and she had become used to being hungry and wearing cast-off clothes.'
Her Father's Sins

There had been need of a soup kitchen before, in the 1840s, and Beattie records that in 1826 and again in 1847 a visitor system had had to be organised to rescue the truly starving – public officers winkling out the worst hit, but 1862 would be Blackburn's nadir, its worst depression, and finally, the town began to prepare itself:

The newly elected Mayor of Blackburn, Mr R. H. Hutchinson, had anticipated that great distress and trouble would manifest itself in the coming winter. To this end, it had been agreed that the sum of two hundred pounds would be set aside for distribution to the growing number of needy by the clergy and ministers of the town. But, meanwhile, a meeting of the textile manufacturers had resulted in the drastic step of closing down even more establishments, the consequence of which was to throw an even greater number of operatives into the ever-increasing ranks of the unemployed. Not a man was safe in his work and though Emma's heart bled for those families already living in fear, she also felt desperately concerned for her husband. Gregory Denton was a changed man. Whereas he had once gone to work of a morning with a spring in his step and a warm kiss for Emma, he now left without a word of farewell and with his face gravely serious. His stooped figure went down the street as though he was approaching the hangman rather than his place of work.

Want bound people together in the seemingly impossible task of survival. Marcia may be talking of the 1930s' depression in *Angels Cry Sometimes*, but the point is just as valid for the 1860s:

It had often struck her that desperate need, for all its horrors, had a strange way of binding folks together, increasing their appreciation of one another and, as a result, there had emerged a kinship between the folk hereabout that was strong and comforting. They were a hard-living courageous folk, whose profound strength and faith helped them to live each day as it came, to forge new friendship and to cherish the old. If one suffered, they all suffered.

The unification of the people in suffering encouraged the poetic infusion of working-class culture, the worker poets in the first place exalting their sense of duty to the mill, for example by calling on operatives to work out their contracts even in the face of personal monetary loss, as in Henry Yates's dialect poem of this era, 'Never Mind 'em' –

...Werk yo'r contract eawt like men
  If yo've signed 'em
If yo loyse bi th' jobs, wod then?
  Never mind 'em.
Werk for t'best, for t'best is sure,
  Whether yo werk for t'rich or poor;
An' if misfortunes knock at th' door,
  Never mind 'em.

This altruism seems extraordinary in hindsight, given the way the mill workers had been exploited and would in future years be let down. Yet the era is important in highlighting this element in the working class character and bringing it to the fore in the mythology of 'the working class hero'. Also, poverty is exalted for itself and given a place of respect, as in 'The Honest Poor', a poem by Hugh Gardiner Graham, a Scotsman by birth, but resident in Blackburn from 1863, this period of terrible depression –

Want bound people together in the seemingly impossible task of survival, and the street urchins evinced this as well as most.

'It was when the carriage was making its way up Town Hall Street and on to King William Street that Caleb Crowther's searching eyes were drawn to the kerbside. There was something disturbingly familiar about the thin, dark-haired ragamuffin...'
Vagabonds

There's honour in the poor man's breast more dear to him than gold;
There's loving kindness in his heart; there's truth and courage bold...
There's resolution in his soul to brave life's toilsome way...

Contemporary poets refer to 1861, the start of the American Civil War, as the onset of the 'Cotton Panic'. So many were inspired to verse in this period that John Baron coined their work 'Poetry of the Panic'.

William Billington, born in Samlesbury in 1827, was pre-eminent in this 'school' and at various times 'a doffer, a stripper and grinder, a weaver and a taper'. A doffer removes and replaces bobbins from spinning machines, a stripper empties bobbins of unused thread, which is sent for waste, a taper minds a dry taping machine. There are many uses for a grinder, but none specific to the textile industry.

Being poor, Billington was educated at Sunday School, though later he attended classes at the Mechanics' Institution in Blackburn. His lot, like Jo's, was '...cast amid the lowly masses –

One can talk and write about poverty and never quite understand what it means to live in a world in which even the most basic things don't figure. What brought it home to me was Jo's comment that they didn't have cups in the house, only jam-jars or milk bottles to drink out of, and, when I asked her where the title of Cradle of Thorns *came from, her saying, 'I was looking for the feeling of how it was. Now, my younger brother, when he was born, I was about five, and I remember vividly my mother bringing him home from hospital and his cradle was an orange box lined with newspaper in front of the fire. That came to me while I was thinking about that book.'*

Whose joy and sorrows I full oft have sung
And through the glooms which cloud the working classes
Some feeble gleams of sunshine may have flung.

Two volumes by Billington, 'Sheen and Shade' and 'Lancashire Songs', were published twenty-two years apart, in 1861 and 1883, due to the fact that the people of Blackburn were too poor to buy books in the intervening years. His two poems, 'Blackburn As It Is' and 'The Cry of the Crowd' breathe the very spirit of lament that characterised the human contours of the town at this time. Writing from personal experience, unblighted by intellectual or any other pretension, he finds his way unimpeded to the point:

I have battled with Want
  For a terrible term,
And been silent, till silence seemed crime,
  Yet I mean not to rant,
But will yield you a germ
  Of plain truth in an unpolished rhyme...

1900, showing the working-class costume at this time, when the workers, like Blackburn weaver-poet, William Billington, were beginning to cry, 'Fraud!'

By 1902, however, the dichotomy of the wealthy mill owner and his impoverished worker, carefully masked, as we shall see, in the formative years of revolution, is now painfully evident to the workforce, and in that year, when George Hull was making Henry Yates's poem, 'Never Mind 'em', part of his collection, he is able to declare that there are very few operatives left in Blackburn who would work out their contracts in the face of monetary loss.

Stripped of his autonomy, independence and tradition, cast into poverty and misery to make a handful of mill owners rich, the Blackburn weaver was *finally* beginning to lay duty aside and speak out, as here, in William Billington's seminal poem, 'Fraud, The Evil of the Age':

With what unutterable shame and scorn,
Humiliation and indignant rage,
The bosom of the honest man is torn
Who contemplates the evils of this age –

Position and name of The Feilden's Arms at Mellor Brook tells of a major takeover in the early days of the revolution, which set up the Feilden family as sole lords of the Manor of Blackburn. It stands close to the site of Woodfold Hall, Mellor, which Henry Sudell, a millionaire from cotton at 56, built in 1798. When Sudell went bust seven years later, the Feilden family snapped up Sudell's share of Blackburn.

The Spirit of Industry

So what took the working man so long? Given the poverty and degradation into which so many fell in the 19th century, why didn't the Blackburn cotton worker flex his muscles about poor wages and living and working conditions earlier? Why was it, after the hand-loom workers failed to halt the mechanisation of the industry, Blackburn became, in Derek Beattie's words, 'one of the most peaceful of weaving towns right up to 1914'?

The story of how the mill masters got away with so much is tragic because it turns on the exploitation, painstakingly deliberate, of the heroic, resolute, unyielding character that we have associated with the tradition of Blackburn spinners and weavers since the beginning, a character which, as their fate unfolded before them, kept many obdurately optimistic until the end.

Far from there being a 'them and us' mentality in Blackburn in the 19th century there was a 'one of us' mentality, encouraged by a mill-owner understanding and manipulation of the tradition from which their workers' character came. Perversely, the mill owners understood the tradition because it was their tradition too.

Right from the start the revolution was masterminded by ordinary people, who, like the domestic hand-loom workers, were *of* the land. The Manor of Blackburn ceased to be in the hands of the

The Feildens, whose association with Blackburn preceded their 1721 purchase of a third share of the Manor of Blackburn by 150 years or so, were based at the 400-acre estate of Witton Park (to the west of Blackburn, where the Blakewater meets the Darwen – above*), the original house being replaced by Witton House in 1800, itself demolished in 1954.*

Originally the Feildens were of yeoman not aristocratic birth, and the revolution for the first time brought many of common birth to the fore. For example in the 1780s a man called Horsfield was worth less than five shillings, but by the 1830s he had made £300,000 from cotton, a fortune in those days.

aristocracy in 1721, after Thomas Belasyse Viscount Falconbergh sold out to three men who came originally of yeoman stock (free-holder families of common, not aristocratic birth) – William Baldwin, Henry Feilden and William Sudell. By and by, Baldwin sold out to the Feildens, who, with the Sudells, became instrumental in the transformation of the Blackburn cotton industry.

In 1798, Henry Sudell had more hand-loom operatives working for him than anyone in the area and called the tune for all merchant manufacturers, who had to match or undercut his terms or lose their operatives to him. But no-one would be immune from risk in the industrialisation of the world, however early in its inception, and in 1827 Sudell fell from millionaire to bankrupt after a failed foreign speculation. So the Feildens swallowed him up, too. There is still a pub, close to the original base of the Sudells, north of Blackburn at Mellor Brook, called The Feilden's Arms.

The Feildens lived to the west of Blackburn at Witton Park, and with sole control of the Manor they went from strength to strength, continuing to own some 2,000 acres of Blackburn into the 1880s and dispensing their largess by founding the local technical

Looking up 18th-century Paradise Lane to the 20th-century Technical College building, valuable legacy of the revolution, originally founded in 1888 by courtesy of the Feilden family, the foundation stone laid by the Prince and Princess of Wales, later King Edward VII and Queen Alexandra.

college, re-establishing the 16th-century Queen Elizabeth's Grammar School, and, as we have already seen, by granting Blackburn the 50-acre Corporation Park.

These families had been small freeholders. They could relate to the rural values of their workers. Moreover, not only were they *of* the land, but once they had made their money, they returned to it, and in this they set the mould for mill owners into the future.

Typically, as a mark of his success, a mill owner would move out of town and emulate the life of the rural squire. Indeed this whole squirearchical theme permeated the cotton mill scene. For, just as the village squire owned the lives of his villagers, so the mill owner owned the lives of his factory operatives. In Blackburn, as indeed in many rural squirearchies throughout the nation, it worked well, without resentment, everyone knowing their place.

In the early days, the owners came from the ranks of merchants who had facilitated the domestic weaving system. Unlike the putter-out, the merchant's contacts and buying and selling expertise had not been made redundant by the mechanisation of industry. Eventually, others with an eye to the main chance, men with genuine working-class status, came up through the industry to join them. They found their feet despite not having the merchants' ready money because, at the start, it wasn't a capital-intensive business. Machine manufacturers were only too happy to extend generous terms of credit in order to establish themselves.

Leonard Horner, a factory inspector, writes in 1837 about a mill owner called Horsfield who had risen from the working classes and made a fortune of £300,000, which most certainly was a fortune in those days, but couldn't write his own name: 'He told me that at 18 years of age [in the late 1780s] he had not five shillings in the world beyond his weekly wages of 15 shillings. Out of his wages he saved £28, bought a spinning jenny and made £30 the first year. In 1831 he made £24,000 of profit. He employs 1,200 people. He is not a solitary case; there are many not unlike him in this part of the country.'

Gradually there arose an in-crowd, mill-owner scene, a club whose members took over positions of power in the town, the best of them managing to do this while giving the impression of still being one of the people. Money was not enough in itself to ensure membership of the club. Derek Beattie tells how the brewer Daniel Thwaites was at one time Blackburn's richest man, but he remained an outsider, a non-member of the in-crowd club, even after he became an MP.

It was of course a cotton club. You had to be in cotton. You also had to have money, but not shout about it. New-money arrogance and pretension would not win you membership. You also had to evince, or at least indulge, the character of 'a gradely mon' – honest, straight and fair, stoical principle, pride in your work, for that was what gained you respect with the workers and ensured a loyal power base.

'Mr Harry, the owd 'un, the gam' cock.'

Harry Hornby was both a full member of the club and a Blackburn MP for a long period up to 1910. As Beattie writes: 'Hornby typified the kind of man that the people of Blackburn admired and looked up to. He was known locally as "Mr Harry", the "owd 'un" or "the gam' cock". He personified the qualities most respected in Blackburn society. He had little knowledge of affairs outside the borough... yet when necessary he knew just what he stood for and stuck to his beliefs.'

The Tudor-built Pleasington Old Hall on the Pleasington Estate on which Sir Harry Hornby lived, his house demolished in 1932 to make way for Pleasington Cemetery.

When a mill owner like Hornby stood for office, he sought support not where he lived, but in the area of his mill, among his people. Beattie tells of cotton workers pinning the colours of their master to their machines. Worker loyalty to the mill was akin to football fan and club. A team spirit was encouraged by inter-mill games of football, brass bands and the like. Looking for comparison today, one thinks of the 20th-century anthemic culture of corporate Japan. Workers and mill owners in Blackburn shared the same values, the same work ethic, they shared the same tradition... *didn't they?*

Binding this supposed shared loyalty was a 'Blackburn against the world' philosophy, for what happened outside Blackburn had no relevance at all. There was a carefully worked, inward-looking focus on your mill, your street, your pub. Also, the town's insularity was celebrated in a kind of political *omerta* in Westminster, a tradition of silence among Blackburn MPs. They simply would not speak. Harry Hornby managed never to utter a single word in Parliament in twenty-three years as a backbencher. Memories scored with recent images of Blackburn politicians, Barbara Castle,

Jack Straw (who is not in fact of the area), may find this scarcely credible. The strategy sealed Blackburn off from distracting influences and encouraged indifference to what was going on outside, the divisive them-and-us mentality that characterised the industrial scene elsewhere.

Jo's sense of a 'closed-in' environment, noted earlier, seems all of a sudden more than architectural!

This hold that mill owners exercised over the working classes brought about an overwhelmingly Conservative workforce. Tiplady became Chairman of the Blackburn Operative Conservative Association and his 1839 Annual Statement evinces a widespread feeling among workers: 'At this period of time there is no need of lengthened argument to demonstrate the vast importance of Societies like ours, whether to the members thereof, as furnishing them with a shield against the dangerous theories and seductive mischief of falsely-called "Liberalism", or to the community at large, attending to preserve a sound heart and an honest spirit in those who are the very thews and sinews of our State – the upright, industrious, independent artisans of Britain.'

So noticeable was worker compliance that as late as 1900, the Blackburn Tory party was accused of *buying* votes 'by means of the beer barrel'. Clearly pressure was exerted at various levels. For example, the Blackburn poet and grocer Robert Clemesha had his rent increased by £15 a year by his landlord, John Fleming, upon discovering that he did not intend to vote Tory at the time of the 1832 Reform Bill.

The Second Reform Act, in 1867, increased the number of Blackburn voters by a factor of five, but the new electorate, swelled by the working class, happily voted in a Tory.

So marked was the Tory allegiance in the workforce by 1932 that Oswald Mosley selected Blackburn to launch his British Union of Fascists, marching through the town with his black-shirt followers, believing the workers to be susceptible to coercion from the far Right. But he had misread the tenor. Blackburn spinners and weavers were not Right-wing extremists. What guided them was their tradition, a resolute work ethic and sense of duty, a tradition that came from way back. They no more belonged to the loony Right than the loony Left. They were *a*political. What they stood for were their ideals, which the mill masters shared...*didn't they?*

Even into the 20th century in Blackburn, long after William Billington wrote 'Fraud, The Evil of the Age', and even after the bleakest depressions of the 1920s and '30s, there was endless optimism that things would get better, endless resolve among the mill workers. William Woodruff shakes his head sadly, but in awe, at his father, forced out of work by industrial depression, trailing off each morning to nearby towns, avoiding men that would beat him up for being a 'knobstick' (a strike breaker) and joining crowds in the hope of being taken on. Woodruff's sister, Brenda, was less charitable, referring to him as 'a gaumless creature. He had the head and brains of a brass knob. He didn't foresee anything because he never thought about anything. He was a grand worker, nobody better, but where brains were concerned he was lost.'

He, like millions of others, could not imagine himself outside the class into which tradition confined him – 'confined' because, sadly, his tradition had ceded autonomy and independence, the right to think for oneself, though the need to do so became increasingly clear. When finally the workers cried, 'Fraud,' as they watched the wealthy mill owners retreating to their country houses, their concept of 'duty' – 'Owd Peter ne-er his duty shirk'd' – changed acrimoniously to a demand for 'rights!', a position we have yet to get beyond.

There is, throughout Jo's *oeuvre*, a sense of this duty, though often it comes with one leaving another their duty to perform. In *Looking Back*, Molly Tattersall gives up her fiancé, Alfie Craig, to look after her six brothers and sisters when her mother leaves her father, Frank. In *Her Father's Sins*, Queenie realises, she will 'have to grow up quickly in order to take care of Aunt Biddy,' and when Biddy dies, her sense of duty extends to cleaning up her father's drunken vomit and generally looking after him, finally, to

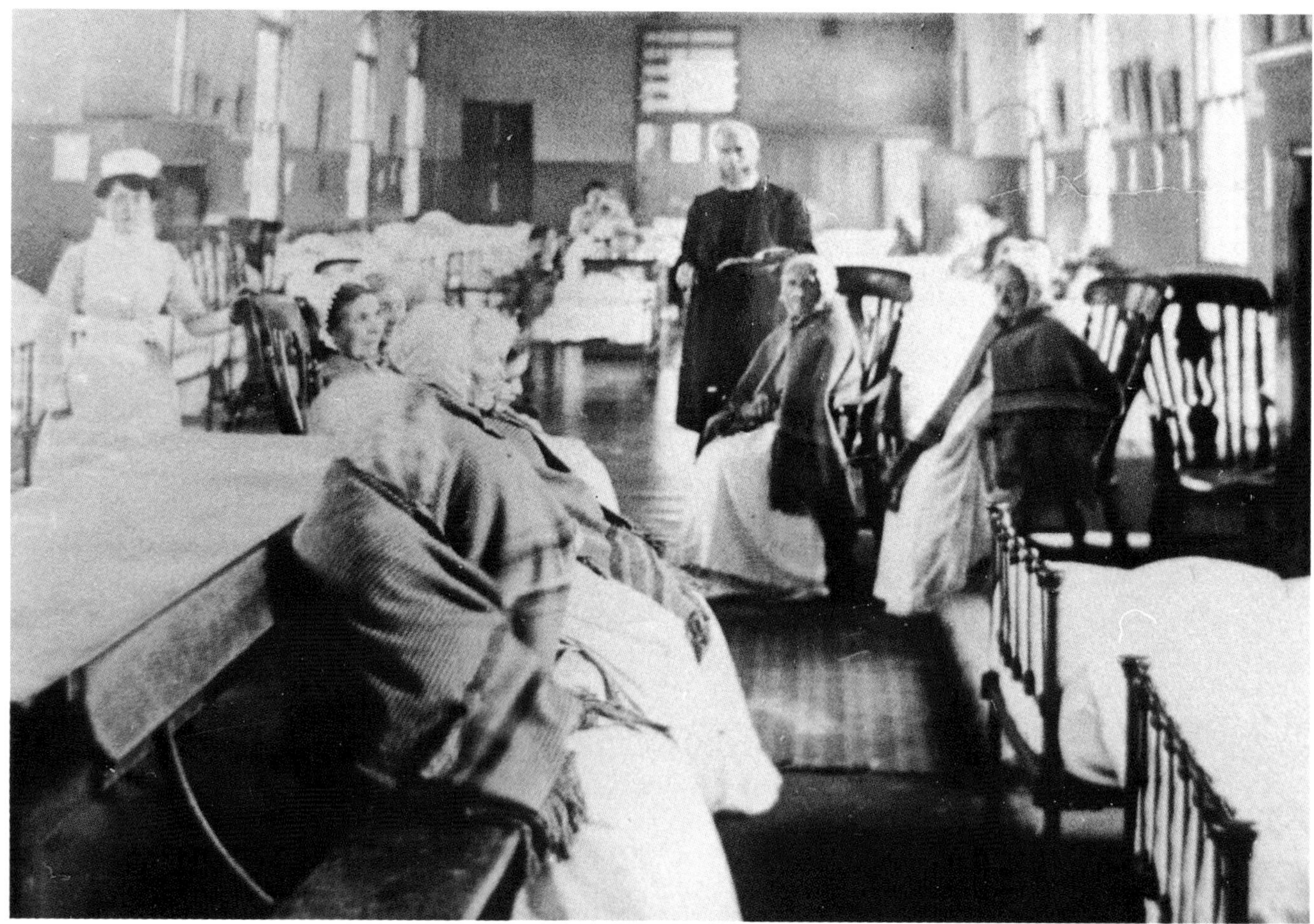

The workhouse hospital ward. Fear of the Workhouse was rife. 'None of the other children in the street had been allowed to play with Phoebe on account of her father being an assistant at the workhouse mortuary. "He smells of death," the parents would say, their two great fears in life being the workhouse and then the mortuary.' Jessica's Girl

be raped by him. In *Born To Serve*, Elizabeth Marshall recognises a duty to love the child who is saying that she is pregnant by her father. For men, work was seen as a duty first, only later was it deemed a right. It was demoralising to be put out of work as well as materially impoverishing. In *Tomorrow The World*, Silas Little, the best tailor in Blackburn, believes that responsibility binds us all, and 'the only way we can survive is by learning to love it as if it were part of our very soul.'

Silas learns to love it so well that he dies working late into the night at his table.

In the 19th century the mill masters did all they could to affirm and encourage these traditional principles, which, to their great advantage, placed pride in one's work and duty dead centre and gave the worker, if not much money, hard-won dignity and self-respect.

Thereafter, theirs was a strategy of non-adversarial management, of pre-empting worker strife, of implementing reforms that cost nothing and gave the distinct impression that they cared.

The Blackburn mill owners sweetened exploitation with paternalism, always careful to underwrite the worker traditions in order to milk their work-orientated values. This made a for a 'flexible' strategy, so that, for example, child workers could benefit if it meant avoiding more stringent factory reform. The result was an illusion of altruism conjured out of the most exploitive situation imaginable, disinterested worker values serving the self-interest of the entrepreneurial mill owners.

For example, vigorous support of legislation limiting child working hours pre-empted a more far-reaching factory reform lobby, which occurred elsewhere, but not in Blackburn, in the 1830s.

A decade or so later, unions would start to form, but the mill masters became past masters at avoiding confrontation. They gained positions on committees and organisations pressing for change, eventually to control them. They instituted the Standard List – standard rates of pay for all jobs throughout all the mills in Blackburn, thereby removing a key platform of union power. In 1834, the year when six farmworkers were sentenced to seven years penal servitude for forming a trade union in a village called Tolpuddle in Dorset – the Tolpuddle Martyrdom was a key event in trades union history – the Blackburn mill masters actually joined forces with their workers over the New Poor Law.

The law was a milestone in a series of Acts designed to relieve poverty, but it turned on the principle that relief should not be so benevolent as to encourage people not to work. 'Every penny bestowed that tends to render the condition of the pauper more eligible than that of the independent labourer is a bounty on indolence and vice,' argued the commissioners with something of a modern ring.

Fear of the workhouse was palpable, and Blackburn poet William Gaspey railed in his poetry against the 'Modern Star-Chamber' which the Poor Law legislation set up. In 'The Victim' he denounces the law for making the mother – not the father – responsible for the maintenance of an illegitimate child, summoning support for his theme with the heart-rending image of a pauper 'in the convulsive agonies of death', shielding 'her infant from the cutting blast' and calling with her last breath, 'God protect my child!' For nobody else would...except the Blackburn mill masters... *wouldn't they?*

Elsewhere, townships set about herding the unemployed into workhouses, splitting up families at the door, making life for the unemployed as unpleasant as possible, and driving a wedge between society and the unemployed. Poverty was for the first time a stigma, *by law*. But in Blackburn, aware how strong feelings were running, the mill masters seized the opportunity to further their all-for-one philosophy. They openly flouted the new law, continuing to extend relief to impoverished families outside the workhouse system, and the strategy put them in good stead to deal with the first big test of master-worker solidarity, which came between 1838 and 1850, when the Chartists made a national rallying call to the new industrial working class.

A charter for social equality was drawn up at national level. Electoral reform was touted as the first step to securing it. Universal suffrage was one of its six principles and came in response to the Reform Bill of 1832, which had merely given votes to the middle class.

Support was strong in the Midlands and the North, but in Blackburn, disarmed by the mill masters' recent opposition to the New Poor Law, the mill workers paid little heed. A call to strike in 1839 was ignored completely, and the *Blackburn Standard* praised Blackburn workers for their *co-operative spirit* and for the value they attached to the 'spirit of industry'.

In 1842, however, there *were* problems, though it is instructive to see how they came about. 'On 6th August,' Tiplady writes in his diary (which is not always easy to read), 'commenced one of the most extraordinary and complete turnouts which has ever occurred in this Kingdom; it began at Stapley Bridge, on a question of wages relative to a proposed deduction of 2d for cash from the most unprincipled Master connected with the Anti-Corn Law League. [The Anti-Corn Law League was an organisation founded in 1839 to oppose the restriction of foreign imports made legal by the Corn Laws.] This deduction was attempted at a time when the Trade, which had been depressed [was making] a healthy revival, and so exasperated the Operatives that they refused to go to work altogether.'

On August 15 rioting workers were prevented from entering a mill by, Tiplady records, 'a detachment of the 72nd Highlanders under the command of Lieut. Col. Arbuthnot. Fifteen prisoners were taken... In the meanwhile straggling gangs of ten or twelve took the advantage of surprising different Mills in the Town and with the exception of about four the whole were closed before night. Foiled in the general attempts...the mob retired for the day and threatened a descent of more violent and determined characters on the following morning. Accordingly, they appeared in great strength on the Accrington Road and proceeded to the Magistrates having installed in ----- Street a strong police force with a company of the 72nd Highlanders, a troop of the Lancashire Yeomanry Corps and Troops of the 11th Hussars to meet them. They encountered the mob at Further Gate... pursuing them across the fields in every direction. In the course of a few moments they were utterly dispersed and about 75 Prisoners captured, which were lodged in the Barracks for safety.

'By such vigilant means the Town and Neighbourhood was saved from pillage and other

Old hand-loom weavers cottages in Further Gate, east of Salford Bridge, which were involved in the riots of 1842. 'A strong police force with a company of the 72nd Highlanders, a troop of the Lancashire Yeomanry Corps and Troops of the 11th Hussars encountered the mob at Further Gate... pursuing them across the fields in every direction.'

violations of the Law, – yet on the following day the soldiers were obliged to fire on the mob, and several persons were severely wounded, but happily not mortally – the most serious case was that of a young woman living in Penny Street who happened to be returning home from the Mill at the time the discharge of the firearms took, and unfortunately two Bulls struck her and it was thought there was little chance of recovery. It is highly to the credit of the Regimental Surgeon and officers of the Right as well as the Surgeons resident in the Town, that the poor innocent victim was promptly and gratuitously attended. – Medicine and Nourishment were ---- administered ---- with good success, as ---- to this time (Nov. 28th) the young woman survives, and is doing extremely well.'

Beattie reports that eleven strikers were transported to Tasmania and some fifty-eight sent to prison. According to Tiplady,

Cherry Tree, part of 'that enviable outer area of Blackburn', to which the middle classes began to retreat as the gulf between 'them' and 'us' was at last made clear.

the uprising occurred when a foolish mill master demanded a wage reduction for political purpose and at a time when business was good. That had been the fatal tactical mistake, but the riot would not have been so serious if the force of Blackburn workers had not been swelled by incoming Chartist strikers from Manchester and Stalybridge. It is unlikely that they will have been especially welcome. Certainly, not much more was heard of Chartism in Blackburn henceforth.

Worker riots were, indeed, unusual in the town, as was the use of force to quell unrest. A more typical response from the resourceful industrialists came in 1845, when mill owners sorted out a demo by treating 1,000 activists to tea.

This unique management-worker relationship was largely maintained until late in the 19th century when takeovers and

The mill masters had been rumbled, but what could the workers do about it?

The answer came in May 1878. A crowd of 5,000 ran riot from Blackburn to Clayton Manor in Wilpshire and fired the house of Colonel Robert Raynsford Jackson, Chairman of the Textile Employers' Federation.

amalgamations of mills began to dilute worker loyalty to one master, and the mill masters themselves began to retreat to their mansions on the fringe of the town, leaving a new, lower middle-class managerial level to administer their businesses for them. This engendered resentments, the new men were not looked up to in quite the same way as those who had forged the industrial revolution in the first place. These were pen pushers, not hands-on entrepreneurs. Heroes were made of more adventurous stuff.

What had riveted the 'spirit of industry' into the hearts of the workers had disappeared. It was no longer 'one for all and all for one'. Their fellow travellers had deserted them, the masters had used their ticket out. Suddenly, the gulf between 'them' and 'us' was made clear. This is the period that produced William Billington's worker-awareness poem, quoted above, 'Fraud, The Evil of the Age'.

The mill masters had been rumbled, but what could the workers do about it?

The answer came in May 1878. Following an insensitive wage cut of 10%, 20,000 of them came out on strike. A crowd of 5,000 ran riot from Blackburn to Clayton Manor in Wilpshire, the house of Colonel Robert Raynsford Jackson, Chairman of the Textile Employers' Federation. He and his family managed to escape in a brougham, but the house was fired and gutted – damage to the tune of £12,000 was caused – and the rioters dragged a burned-out four-wheeled carriage back to Blackburn as a trophy. The following day the windows of sixty-four houses in middle-class Preston New Road were smashed. Troops were called out and the workers' leader, a man called Smalley, was sentenced to fifteen years of penal servitude. There were eight other jail sentences – from eight to fifteen years. It was a humiliating defeat, and deepened the sense of worker enslavement.

Twelve years later, Blackburn's Chamber of Commerce warned of the dangers of the town having only one string to its bow – cotton. Blackburn would stand or fall with the cotton industry, and there were worrying signs of it doing the latter.

After the First War (1914-'18) there was a short-lived mini-boom, but in the 1920s and '30s the downward spiral began, and it was dramatic. Foreign competitors had used the war to supply Blackburn's traditional markets, and, in a clear display of loss of control at the helm, Blackburn sold them the machinery to do it. Crucial to the industry had been exports to India of Blackburn Greys. Between 1913 and 1936 these exports were reduced by more than 80%. By the 1920s, India, China and Japan had snaffled Blackburn's trade for themselves. Unable to obtain Blackburn cloth during the war, India had looked to its own industry, and Blackburn had actually sold them the machines to tool up, the town's Technical College proudly training overseas students in the textile skills in which it specialised.

In *The Road to Nab End*, William Woodruff writes of the hunger and poverty in Blackburn following the Crash of 1920, of his father, in desperation, taking in mail bags to sew and mending clogs. The day his father scrubbed the Victoria monument in Blackburn he describes as the bleakest of the Great Depression. Under the National Insurance Act of 1920 Woodruff's father received fifteen shillings a week for fifteen weeks, his mother five shillings for a shorter period. There were also benefits from the trade union, but they soon ran out.

The 'pop shop' (the pawn) then came into its own, as Jo describes in *Angels Cry Sometimes*:

If there was one shop Marcia could never walk by without pressing her nose to the window, it would have to be Billy's pawn shop. This Aladdin's cave was easily identifiable from a great distance by the three enormous brass spheres which protruded stiffly from a sturdy bracket above the doorway. Now, she and Polly surveyed the numerous articles laid out in the window; rings, musical instruments, shoes, false teeth and paraphernalia of all shapes and description. All of these items represented a varying degree of heartache and sacrifice for their owners, who brought their precious belongings to Billy when times became so hard that their only salvation was to pawn perhaps a treasured brooch or a Sunday-best one and only suit, for a few paltry pence. A more valuable article such as a wedding-ring might produce the staggering sum of four shillings. The problem lay in recovering the goods, which called not only for the production of the sum lent, but a handsome interest charge for Billy's trouble as well....

The last time, it took Marcia almost three months to get [her coat] back, and that had been dangerously close to the 'keeping limit', before the goods were sold off.

The coat was really nothing special by other folks' standards, Marcia mused, nevertheless feeling really good in it... but to her, it was something to be treasured, kept for out-of-the-ordinary occasions, like today for instance. The feel of the soft brown wool against her skin, and the way the material gathered in at the tiny waist and buttoned sleeves, always made her feel elegant. A wry little smile lit up her lovely dark features as she glanced down at the shabbiness of her 'best' grey lace-up boots, and thought on her long black hair stuffed unglamorously beneath the black cloche hat which had been old Ma

Women grading coal in 1932 and leaving little doubt as to the morale of the workforce by this time.

After the First War there was a short-lived mini-boom in cotton and those other industries, like coal, which served it, but in the 1920s and '30s the downward spiral began, and it was dramatic.

Bendall's. Hmph! Pity the rest on me couldn't be afforded such elegance, she mused.

Suddenly, everything was realising its true value.

Between 1918 and 1922 the number of looms in operation was cut by a half. A partial recovery in 1924/5 was followed by the General Strike in 1926, abandoned eight days later. Humiliation and victimisation ensued under the auspices of the Trade Disputes and Trade Union Act of 1927, which abolished rights fought for and won by the workers earlier. In 1929 the spinners were locked out to enforce wage reductions. In 1930 it was the weavers turn. By then half the workers in Blackburn were on the streets. In the period 1930-1938 the number of unemployed veered between 21.5% and 47% in the town, and underemployment was as much a problem. Hidden by these figures, bad as they were, was the fact that the cotton industry operated on a piece-work basis. Men were working, and therefore not classified as unemployed, but were not earning enough to live.

The output of industry had been halved since 1914 and the number of workers reduced by nine-tenths since before the war. Late in 1931 the cotton industry in Blackburn reached the point of collapse: 'Father was smashing looms with a sledgehammer

Posing in a Blackburn street, 1933, in the midst of Depression. This, then, was the situation that met Jo's parents when they first arrived in Derwent Street and started a family.

which he had earlier tuned with all the skill of a piano-tuner,' writes Woodruff.

When Mahatma Gandhi, the Indian political and spiritual leader and social reformer, visited England for political talks in the same year, he was invited to Blackburn to see for himself the misery that his industrial policy, which had banned cloth imports from Britain, was causing. *The Lancet*, the British journal of the medical profession, reported that people in Blackburn were literally dying of starvation. Gandhi, with experience of worse poverty in India, was not impressed: 'The poverty I have seen distresses me,' he was quoted as saying, 'but compared to the poverty and pauperism of the starving millions of India, the poverty of Lancashire dwindles into insignificance.' In October of the following year, 1932, a hunger march to London was given a rousing send-off in the market square.

This, then, was the situation that met Jo's parents when they arrived in Derwent Street and started a family. Indeed, Jo's mother claimed to remember Mahatma Gandhi's visit – 'Gandhi killed it off. Mum said, "That's Gandhi's fault, all our cotton mills closing."' He

In the 1940s and '50s and right up to the 1960s there was no bathroom or indoor toilet in 40% of Blackburn homes, whereas in Manchester, just a few miles to the south, 200 acres of the worst slums had already been cleared by 1939.

bought all the machines.' There is mention of his visit in both *Let Loose The Tigers* and *Angels Cry Sometimes*:

The decade did see one or two alternative moves to stem the widespread depression. In 1936, Blackburn's first industrial estate started up, an electronics firm its first tenant, and Thwaites and Dutton's hung in there. But nothing could take up the slack left by cotton. By 1937 the number of power looms had been reduced to 37% of the boom-time total. The number rose a little after the Second War, when there was again a mini-boom, and then steadily declined from 1956 on.

During this period, however, there were some improvements nationally. In 1942 the Beveridge Report determined to make 'want under any circumstances unnecessary' and laid out the basis of a social-security system. In 1948 the National Health Service was set up to be financed mainly by taxation. By then, typhoid and cholera had been stamped out. The medics had as good as got rid of that other scourge, rickets, and the death rate from tuberculosis was being lowered year on year.

Still, however, in the 1940s and '50s and right up to the

1960s there was no bathroom or indoor toilet in 40% of Blackburn homes, whereas in Manchester, just a few miles to the south, 200 acres of the worst slums had already been cleared by 1939: 'We built blocks of flats on the cleared sites, which not long before had been teeming slums,' reported the Manchester Council in 1947, noting advisedly, 'but building on old slum sites cuts two ways. Though the flats are new, the districts are old and overcrowded, as many people had to live in the new flats as used to live in the old slums. You do not always improve things by cramming people in layers on top of one another instead of spreading them out sideways with more space.'

This was not a lesson Blackburn learned immediately. The town's two-decade clearance plan included the replacement of Larkhill with the tower blocks still in evidence today and brought a cry for a stay of execution from townspeople, who didn't want their terraced-house communities destroyed. In *Her Father's Sins*, Rick Marsden's father has an interest in the post-war slum clearance programme in Blackburn. The programme was halted for a while and the overall strategy modified to include grants for renovation of existing dwellings, but Jo's Derwent Street community was laid waste, and Henry Street disappeared in a wholesale clearance and re-build of the town centre. Plans were unveiled to take down the clock tower and cover the market with a new shopping precinct in 1955, at the very moment that her mum took the family into exile.

By then, the so-called 'spirit of industry' was all but dead. Millions had been made and lost and salted away. The workers had been well and truly done. Richard Oestler had got it about right for a hundred years when, in 1830, he found, 'Slavery, and harder Bondage than the Negroes in our English plantations in America.'

One can talk of tradition and of the character of the northern working class, obdurate in the face of the big rip-off, and too easily forget that the revolution broke many a family and drove more to drink. At the lowest end of Blackburn society, character was constantly degraded by a combination of poor education, want and drink, even from the start. In 1835, the vicar of Blackburn, Reverend John Whittaker, wrote of the Blackburn underclass: 'Their immorality in every respect, their gross, filthy habits, their ruffian-like brutality beggar all description. The Sabbath breaking and drunkenness are dreadful. The beer shops have increased the latter to a frightful extent.' The chaplain of Preston prison could only agree: 'There is a greater proportion of the uneducated classes in Blackburn than in Preston and the passion for liquor is a source of ruin and disgrace...'

By 1862 there was one drink outlet for every twenty-three houses in Blackburn. 'Do you wonder that most people tried to forget the long hours of work and the misery of their homes by going to the only places of warmth and amusement, the taverns and gin palaces?' questioned one observer. Jo writes in *Her Father's Sins* that ninety years on, 'It was an undisputed fact – which any real red-blooded Lancastrian would relate with chest-bursting pride – that there were more pubs, under the colourful names of Bells, Brown Cows, Navigations, and Jug and Bottles, than there were shops.' But the effect this had on life at home was dreadful, as 7-year-old Queenie saw:

Queenie looked around the room. By the look of it, she thought George Kenney's cronies must have turned up with more booze after she'd gone to sleep. Strewn from one end of the oilcloth to the other, empty bottles and jugs had trickled their last sediments into small pools of dark brown stain. There wasn't an ornament left standing upright anywhere on the sideboard, and somebody's half-hearted attempt at poking the fire had filled the hearth with black cinders and ash, like a thick dirt carpet.

Over by the scullery door, the stand-chair which normally stood there like a dutiful sentry was toppled over in a most undignified manner. Queenie surmised that some drunken body had made a futile attempt at diving for the back door which led to the outer yard. Futile, because of the considerable deposit of reeking vomit, spread across the chair-legs and surrounding oilcloth.

Queenie had become used to clearing up such a mess.

Prior to 1841, when a police force came to be resident in King Street, law and order was enforced by a parish constable during the day and a 'watch' at night. Lock-ups were instituted at Darwen Bridge and in the cellars of various pubs. I was told by a local that there is still a tunnel leading from the cellar of the Duke of York to the King's Head and thence to the courtyard of the old Magistrate's Court at the bottom of Montague Street. As most of the crime was drink related, pub-keeps probably paid dividends in the business of policing the town. In 1862 it was reported that 282 of 377 crimes reported had been solved, that there were 127 known prostitutes in the Borough, 61 in brothels, 66 in pubs, and that brothels numbered 19.

Drunkenness only relieved the problem of want and dire exploitation when it ended in unconsciousness. Otherwise, and when consciousness returned, it exacerbated it, and caused most of the crime in the town from 1830 on, so that publicans (and licensing hours) became the favourite quarry of officers of the law:

On January 31, 1856, a publican called William Durham complained of being 'dogged like an assassin, hunted and watched like a felon,' in a letter to the *Blackburn Standard*:

'Sir – Some startling outrages – personal attacks with violence – have very recently been committed...between Sunday night and Monday morning, rows of streets were visited by a roving set of blackguards, gardens trampled upon, trees uprooted, shutters broken, knockers wrenched off, and such works of wanton destruction completed as must have occupied the perpetrators a considerable length of time; and all this done without the detection of a single offender. Where were the police? They were looking after the publicans and beersellers, playing at hide and seek in sly corners and dark entries and obscure alley; crouched in back-yards and behind doors, ready of spring upon the unwary ale seller and spirit vendors, for the smallest infraction of the Law.'

It is difficult not to see the huge number of pubs in the town as the final solution in the pacifying strategy of the mill masters, who owned many of them and rarely built them beyond the mill-worker colonies. In the enslavement process of the Blackburn working man, drink was the effective lobotomy. Tragically, because drink does not relieve humiliation, and because pubs were a male preserve and drinking got bound up with the hard-working, *macho* element in the working man's character, it came to have a terrible effect on the community, and in particular on Blackburn women, when the working man's resentment at his lot was turned on his own family.

'In Blackburn,' wrote J Corin in *Mating, Marriage & the Status of Women*, published in 1910, it is the usual thing for the husband, when he comes home late at night, to give his wife a kicking and beating. The women take it as part of the daily round and don't complain.' Chillingly, in *Somewhere, Someday*, Kelly Wilson, with as much distance of time as Jo, has total recall of what it was like as a child on her tenth birthday in the build-up to such a beating:

'It was my tenth birthday. Mam had made me a wonderful party,' Kelly began. 'Mam baked the cake and dressed it with candles, and all the neighbours came.' Her voice broke with emotion. 'He said I wasn't to have a party, that it was a bloody nuisance.'

She smiled, a sad, childish smile. 'They fought for days ... like they fought about everything she wanted to do.'

Her eyes widened in surprise. 'Somehow she managed to persuade him. He didn't stay, though. He went to the pub. "I won't be back till it's over!" he said, and to be truthful, I didn't want him there. He always spoiled things.'

'At least you got yer party.' Poor as her childhood was, Amy thanked the Lord she had never suffered in the way Kelly had suffered.

'It was the best party ever,' Kelly said softly. 'We laughed and played, and everyone was having a wonderful time. Mam lit the candles on my cake and I couldn't blow them all out at once.' She chuckled then. 'Lenny Parker got excited and blew them all out instead. I didn't really mind, but his mam clouted him round the ear and threatened to take him home if he didn't behave himself.'

A change of mood came over her as she recalled what happened next.

'He came back early, drunk as a lord. "I want this lot out of here," he yelled, and began throwing things about. The children were crying and everyone knew he was out for trouble. In minutes they were all gone; except me and our mam.'

'What about your brother?'

Kelly sighed. 'Michael hid in the scullery as usual.' Reliving the day, she described it in every detail. 'When he began swiping things off the table and smashing them against the wall, Mam shouted for Michael to take me out.' In her mind's eye it was as real as the day it happened, over thirty years ago. 'As we ran through the scullery door, I saw him! He grabbed our mam by the hair and fought her to the ground. I screamed for Michael to help her, but he seemed to be frozen.'

Pausing to take a breath, Kelly wondered if she could go on. It was too real, too alive in her mind.

She heard Amy's voice, soft and persuasive. 'Don't keep it inside,' she said. There's just you and me here, no one else.'

Knowing she could trust her, Kelly went on. 'It had been raining all day, and was still coming down heavy,' she said. 'The yard and cellar were flooded ankle-high as always. Anyway, Michael took me down the steps as far as we could go, and there we sat.' She shivered. 'It was cold, too. The rain soaked us to the skin, but we couldn't go back inside. We daren't.' Closing her eyes, she could hear it all. 'My father was like a crazy thing. We could hear him shouting, things being thrown about, and our mam ...oh, dear God, she sounded terrified. We could hear her cries, "Don't ...please don't".' Here Kelly's voice broke. 'I tried to break away from Michael, but he held me fast, so all I could do was call out to my father. "Leave her alone!" I yelled, over and over. But he took no notice.'

When she faltered, Amy urged, 'Go on, Kelly.'

'Suddenly it all went quiet. We heard the key click in the back door, then a sound from inside, like furniture being shuffled about. I remember Michael telling me to stay where I was, and not to move until he came for me.' Frowning, she momentarily closed her eyes, reading the pictures in her mind. 'He went to the top step and stood on tiptoes, looking through the window. I heard him shout out, then he was banging his fists on the door. "Open this door! Let me in or I'll break it down!" I'd never seen him so agitated. Suddenly the door gave beneath his weight and he was in. "Stay where you are,

The female mill worker above was photographed in 1965, when the number of mills had fallen from a peak of 200 to less than 30, and the number of jobs in the industry had fallen by three-quarters since 1930. On the brighter side, women were 'rebelling at the straitjacket that they'd been placed in,' as Jo put it. Invariably the man of the house was still in charge, but it was less the accepted thing for a husband, when he came home late at night, 'to give his wife a kicking and beating,' as a 1910 report put it, though police figures show that domestic violence remains a dark remnant of the revolution even today.

Kelly!" he yelled. Because I was afraid and confused, I did as I was told.' Putting her hands over her ears, she said, 'I sat very still, with my eyes closed and my hands like this, and I waited.'

The tragic reverberations of this sort of scene are still to be found today. The legend on a set of beer mats sitting on the bar of a pub opposite Burnley police station reads: 'Last year over 18,500 people contacted Lancashire police to report cases of domestic violence.'

In another, fairly modern context (1975, when Jo's novel *Living a Lie* is set), Mildred Marsh berates her brother for beating his wife, Lucinda. All Lucinda had wanted was 'a love as deep and loyal as hers.' In desperation she throws herself under a train, attempting to take her daughter with her.

'Lucinda Marsh was never a tart. She was too attractive for her own good, yes, and she was like a kid at heart. She hated arguments and fighting. She wanted nothing more than to be a good mother and wife, and you made her suffer for it. She was the minnow and you were the shark. You took advantage of her soft nature . . . used her as though she was your personal property. You showed her off to your cronies, then slapped her good and hard if they dared to look at her in a certain way.'

'You don't know what you're talking about.'

'Well, now, that's where you're wrong. Lucinda came to me time and again after you'd beaten her up. She was desperately unhappy, yet still she adored you . . . begged me not to confront you.'

She spat out her next words. 'If any man treated me like you treated her, I'd cut his balls off while he slept!'

Earlier, in Jo's time, in the 1940s and early '50s, women expected a subservient position at home: 'Getting dad's tea ready was the thing,' she remembers. 'He was the *man of the house*. You didn't have anything to eat until he had had what he wanted. If you had anything it would go to the man of the house. Mind you there wasn't anything much to eat except on a Sunday. We only all sat down around the table on a Sunday. There weren't enough chairs, but everything was dragged out to sit around the table.'

The archetypal 'man of the house' in *Angels Cry Sometimes* is, of course, Barty Bendall, who 'drank hard, swore hard, and relentlessly spouted discipline and damnation; ruling his often-servile family with a rod of cast-iron':

The instant Barty Bendall entered the room the atmosphere was charged with fear. An involuntary shiver rippled through Marcia's slim figure, and her expressive dark eyes lost their sparkle. In spite of the forced enthusiasm, her voice was devoid of feeling, perceived only by the ever-watchful Polly. 'Hello Barty. Tea won't be long now,' she told her husband. Looking sharply at Marcia, his whole manner bristling, Barty Bendall grunted acknowledgement.

Wifely compliance meant not only washing and darning and making the man's tea, but waiting up for him when he had been drinking in the pub.

Marcia leaned up on one elbow, fearing, yet half-expecting the worst. 'Drunk!' she whispered into the darkness. 'Blind plaited drunk again, he is!' A rush of nausea swamped her as he continued to shout her name. This was the time she dreaded most – when he came home the worse for drink and demanded the rights of a husband...

There was an almighty crash as something hit the wall in the front room. Barty had fallen against the sideboard, his flailing arms sending the ornaments hurtling to the floor, after which abuse filled the air and Marcia prepared herself for what was coming.

She waited, the thoughts in her mind a whirlpool of disgust and indignation. Her lovely eyes grew morose and dim, as she whispered low, 'A pig. I married a drunken PIG!'

... Shivering, she slithered back into bed where she lay waiting resignedly for the beast now blundering up the stairs, the tears trickling slowly down her lovely face. Her heart thumped with fear: fear of her husband Barty Bendall, and anger at herself for having failed; failed her children, failed at marriage; and most of all, for failing all the happy enthusiastic dreams of her youth.

Turning the tables on the male ego in *Tomorrow The World*, Jo introduces us to the quarryman culture, imagining what it would be like for such a macho man as Tom Mulligan to lose his virility:

The party had gone with a swing. They were merry to a man, and now, with the evening drawing to a close, Tom prepared to leave. 'I'd best be off,' he told the hard-drinking quarrymen. 'The missus hasn't been too well, as you know, and even with Nelly watching over her, it's not right to leave her for too long.' He'd had a good night, and now it was time to go.

'Aye, and I'd best be away an' all,' Dave Grundy declared. 'Me own wife's due to birth any minute. She'd skin me alive if it happened tonight while I were having a bloody good time.'

Laughter greeted his remark, but Ted Louis, a burly fellow with a nasty scar across his lip, had something snide to say. 'We all know about that,' he guffawed, his sly gaze going to Tom, whom he disliked. 'There's not one of us here who ain't fathered a heap o' young 'uns – all except for Tom Mulligan.' His lips curled in a sneer. 'I reckon 'e don't know how to do it right. Happen one of us should show him, eh?'

A terrible silence fell on the party, all eyes on Tom who had turned his face to his tormentor.

Tom Mulligan believes, 'Without pride, a man is nothing!' And, 'with his clothes torn, his face swollen and bloody, one arm hanging limp by his

In the face of the appalling challenges that the revolution offered, worker pride and sense of honour could easily become warped and transformed into egotism.

Turning the tables on the male ego in Tomorrow The World, *Jo introduces us to the quarryman culture, imagining what it would be like for such a macho man as Tom Mulligan to lose his virility. Tom does not handle it well.*

side,' he does manage to salvage his pride, at least in the short-term. But what is the working man's pride becoming? Mulligan refuses his wife the right to question his authority in the home. There is no honour or self-respect in treating a wife the way many of Jo's male characters do. Yet honour and self-respect define pride.

In the face of the appalling challenges that the industrial revolution offered, worker pride and sense of honour could easily become warped and transformed into egotism. Pride is a quiet strength, stoical, even heroic. An egotist, on the other hand, wary of humiliation (as many a working man became), is preoccupied with self-interest. Seeing what he has become leads Tom Mulligan into a moral and emotional *cul de sac*, and suicide seems the only way out:

Jack stood beside Ted, his curious gaze following Ted's stricken stare down into the quarry. Below was the great bucket, filled with sand and ready for raising. Above that was the boom, and hanging from it was Tom Mulligan. 'Oh no!'

Jack cried, his face ashen. 'Dear God, why would he do a thing like that?'

By the time they cut Tom down, it was too late.

The hard work, the exhaustion, the frustration, the humiliation, the indignant rage fired many a Blackburn worker to drink. 'If Barty Bendall could lay claim to anything commendable,' Jo writes in *Angels Cry Sometimes*, 'it was his great capacity for working hard... no one, family nor drinking partners, could deny the truth of it. The greatest pity of it all was that the fruits of his hard labours very rarely served to assist his family in their times of need, rendered even needier by his deliberate neglect.'

Drink kept men like Barty in just the kind of spiral of need that ensured their continued compliance. 'His work was getting him nowhere,' as Jo explained, 'he became "a Jekyll and Hyde" figure, a wonderful man and hard-working, until Friday when he would go to the pub and come home drunk. They all worked hard and they all drank hard on a Friday night.'

So, hand in hand with poverty came drunkenness and domestic violence. 'It was the same for many people. You'd see a man, coming down the street and his wife waiting for him literally with a rolling pin. And there'd be a fight on the street, and she'd shut the door and lock him out. So there was nothing unique about it. It was not peculiar to one family. The man was the boss in his own home.'

At the end of her tether, Jo's mother gathered her children around her in the bus station one day and told them, 'We're leaving...'

3 Broken Hearts

'When mum and dad split, it was quite an awful experience. I cried for weeks. Mum – she was pregnant when she left my dad – she gathered us all together on the bus station, where they used to park the buses over night. She just drew us all together when dad had gone to work. She said she was going to her sister's in Dunstable [Bedfordshire] and she wasn't coming back and she was going to take us all with her. There was a lot of crying – "We don't want to go, we want to stay here..." Me mam wanted to take us all. It was a terrible time. I was fourteen, not a good time. And my two brothers, Bernard and Richard, who come directly after me, they decided to stay with dad. What a decision to have to make when you are 12 or 11 years old! So that was pretty awful. Not only did I miss my friends *and* my dad, but my brothers were left behind too. It was so traumatic, leaving them and my dad behind.'

I asked Jo whether, in the long term, she felt it had been for the best. 'Well, I don't know, because me mam chose another bloke who gave her a bad life. Mam was one of life's casualties, she couldn't choose the right man. She left the boys with dad. He did a wonderful job in bringing those boys up, you know?"

I say that I have noticed that her more recent novels seem less hard on the father figure, and even in the character of Barty Bendall there is a suggestion that maybe Marcia, his wife, was partly to blame, 'She'd tried so hard to hate him... But she found herself pitying him. Had she been to blame in some way?'

'Six of one, half dozen of the other,' said Jo. 'I look back and I think that the bad times were usually weekends, after me dad had had his wages and gone to the pub. He was not a bad man at all, he was a good man, he had a wonderful sense of humour...'

It cannot have escaped readers of Jo's novels that the orphaning of her heroines is a recurring theme, in particular most of them are touched by the loss of the father figure. When, in a telephone conversation with Jo, I suggested that the loss of her father seems to be the source of her inspiration, she was taken aback. 'You know, it is so strange that you say that, because I haven't consciously done that. Though the book that I am working on now – *The Woman Who Left*...you saying that...my god! I have done it again in this book! I never realised I have done that. You are right. How strange.'

Jo paused for a moment, before recalling her father especially warmly. 'He *was* a good man, but he was not demonstrative. That was the thing. He didn't display his feelings towards his children. But towards Winifred he was very, very warm. Not so warm towards me. And all my childhood I can remember thinking, wouldn't it be nice if my dad would put his arms round me and say, "I love you." But he never did.'

Oh, the complexities of the father-daughter relationship, and how especially difficult when part of the character of the northern working class man was not to be emotionally demonstrative. I recalled immediately William Woodruff's story of his father giving a bunch of flowers to his wife, awkwardly, almost abruptly handing them to her, a muffled grunt saying all that could be said.

Barney will have found it doubly difficult to express his feelings for his daughter, who sided so dramatically with her mother. And then Jo brought into the house this story-telling talent, quite foreign to him – 'the last thing he wanted to hear was any of my airy-fairy nonsense,' Jo had said. 'As far back as I can remember I always had that feeling that there was something better than Derwent Street or Henry Street, and that if you worked hard enough you would get there.'

'Maybe he saw and mistrusted that, saw it as a criticism of his way of life,' I said.

'Dad never listened when I told him I wanted to be a writer,' she replied. 'But mum would always encourage me to do what I wanted.'

The sadness was that a weakness for drink could undermine the precious thing that had been won for the working classes in the revolution – what had survived the exploitation – the thing that the mill owners could never get their greedy hands on.

The autonomous, independent tradition of the hand-loom weaver had, over 150 years, been ceded to the industrial revolution, but something had survived, even been strengthened by living in hardship in those closed-in terraces. Jo is specific about what this is in *Don't Cry Alone*, when she writes of Beth Ward: 'Here in Blackburn, with Maisie and her two children, she had found another kind of love, a deep sense of belonging.'

'Belonging to a place, to a street, to a people, to a family is important to you,' I suggest.

'It is *the* most important thing,' she agrees. 'I read about *Angela's Ashes* and Frank McCourt, who came from Limerick, and the people of Limerick denying it was ever like that. They were ashamed of their roots because they had been poor, they had been hungry, and they wanted to forget it because they had done well and had moved on. I cannot understand that attitude.'

'Does that feeling, that "sense of belonging", ever leave you?' I ask.

'No. It is you, it is who you are, it is where you came from. I think every day of my life... I am very aware of how it used to be. Inside I

'That "sense of belonging" is you, it is who you are, it is where you came from. I think every day of my life... I am very aware of how it used to be. Inside I haven't changed a bit. I am still that snotty-nosed kid from the back streets.'

haven't changed a bit. I am still that snotty-nosed kid from the back streets. I have been more fortunate than a lot of people, but my feet are firmly on the ground.'

But drink was also part and parcel of the culture of life in the streets of Blackburn and those that fell victim to it, ensured that they couldn't enjoy this 'belonging' even in their own home. Frank Tattersall in *Looking Back* was such a victim, and his agony is piteous when, with the 'scrawny redhead' he has brought home, he reacts to his wife's letter telling him that she has left him. Molly, their daughter, is in attendance:

Just as she had suspected, the minute she had gone, he picked up the letter and began reading it, his jaw dropping in disbelief as he took in the words.

Molly was halfway up the stairs when she heard him yelling, 'Get out of 'ere, you old hag! Get back to the bloody streets where yer belong!'

Pausing, Molly looked down to see her father manhandling the redhead out the front door. When he saw Molly on the stair, he ordered, 'You! Get back down 'ere this minute.'

Taking her time, she returned to the parlour.

Wild-eyed and furious, Frank flung the offending letter across the table. 'What's all this bloody nonsense then? What game does she think she's playing?'

'It's no game.'

Appearing not to have heard, he gave a nervous little laugh. 'Happen she's heard rumours about them streetwomen who keep following me home.' Pacing up and down, he was like a man demented. 'Well, I'll soon put paid to that, 'cos I'm off to the 'orspital right now, and just let the buggers try and throw me out this time!'

'It's no good you going there.' Molly thought it amazing how the shock of that letter seemed to have sobered him up. 'If you read the letter properly, you'll know she's not there.'

'She's bloody there all right, but not for long, 'cos I'm fetching her back 'ere, where she belongs.'

'You're not listening to me, are you?' Molly had expected him to go berserk and turn the place upside down. Instead, it seemed like all the stuffing had been knocked out of him.

Looking at Molly, he cocked his head to one side, his eyes too bright, his voice beginning to crack. 'Aye, that's what I'll do. Yer mam's had time enough now.' Running his hands frantically through his thinning hair, he said, 'No wonder she's writing silly stuff like that. She'll be going out of her mind in that place. Oh, aye. Once our Amy's home, this damned house might get back to normal.'

When he grabbed up his coat from the sofa Molly cried out to him, 'It's no use you going to the Infirmary. She's not there!'

He paused in the doorway, coat in hand, head bowed and his back to her. 'Don't go fooling yourself,' she told him harshly, hating him. 'Mam's gone, thanks to you, and judging by that letter, she's never coming back.'

For what seemed a lifetime, the silence in the little parlour was unbearable.

Frank remained quite still, head hanging low, coat in hand; neither he nor Molly made a move. In the background the clock ticked and from somewhere upstairs came the creaking of a floorboard.

Laura Blake's regret and sadness at the loss of her father is almost tangible in *Take This Woman*, as is Beth Ward's loss of her father in *Don't Cry Alone*. Beth sees where her father is wrong, but knows that he is a victim of his own misguided perception of life and incapable of doing other than he does:

In that moment before she turned away, Beth glanced lovingly at her father's still body. His eyes were closed, but she could still see the unforgiving look in them – the terrible accusation. The pain was gone from his face, but it was not gone from her heart. She loved him. Nothing would ever change that. She had lost him. But Death had not taken him from her. No. It was nothing so simple as Death that had parted them.

Even when the monster Barty Bendall dies in *Angels Cry Sometimes*, Marcia's sense of loss spills over onto the page a lament to the paradox of love and bitterness that characterised an era, and she absolves him of blame:

As she looked down at the prematurely aged face of Barty Bendall, Marcia reproached herself. The wicked features had relaxed in that quiet moment before his life and his torment were over. 'I'm sorry, Barty,' she murmured, the tears spilling down her face. 'Oh I'm so sorry!'

Happiness is always just around the corner in Jo's stories, as if there hangs a veil between 'what is' and 'what might have been'. So it was for countless families in Blackburn between about 1830 and 1950, whatever the nature of their loss. The novels have helped Jo resolve hers, but should anyone doubt what it has taken to bring her this far, they should listen to Kitty Marsh in *Living a Lie*:

In her dreams she was suffocating, lost in a swirl of dark fog, her lungs hot and burning. Asleep, she fought against it. She opened her eyes but couldn't see. 'DADDY!' The fog tasted sour, forcing itself into her mouth, her body. While her senses weakened, her desperate screams grew louder: 'DADDY, HELP ME!'

Henry Street, 1958, a few years after the family left – Jo's street, wherein the life was lived that became her books, now quite empty. In 1824 the Georgian terrace had been home to professional people, including a lawyer called Dixon Robinson. One hundred and forty years later it was razed to the ground.

Suddenly he was there. 'Don't be afraid,' he told her softly. 'Hold on to me.' Echoes of her mother's voice haunted her. 'You mustn't run away . . . keep hold of my hand.' She was afraid he meant to hurt her too, but she couldn't fight him, she couldn't breathe, 'Please don't kill me, Daddy!' Her eyes closed and she was at his mercy.

So deep ran Jo's feelings that a series of novels, kept separate from her main output, insisted themselves upon her. 'I never intended writing frightening books,' she told me. 'But about six years ago I suddenly started writing under my mother's name [Jane Brindle] and these books are very, very sinister, psychological thrillers. They're dark, sinister books which I never meant to write, but they creep up behind me and push me so hard that eventually I just have to do it. I think those feelings come from my childhood when I was afraid and hungry and emotions ran high between mam and dad.

'There is, in *Scarlet*, a story where the girl is hiding in the dumb waiter. She is absolutely petrified because she can hear her father's feet coming down the stairs, and she knows she is going to get a real good hiding, so she is hiding in there... That was a deep, dark memory. A lady wrote to me and said she had read this scene and her heart was beating ten to the dozen because she was so frightened it was me in that dumb waiter.'

The ultimate reality, however – Ruby Miller's 'silver lining' to the cloud of misery that hung over Blackburn in *Nobody's Darling* – is alive in the mainstream novels, not because Jo is milling a good idea, but because she and her fictional characters embody the spirit of a people and evince this sense of belonging, of tradition. Periodically television soaps and advertisements trade on tradition with a very bastard image. Few draw directly, as Jo does, from the well of experience that makes it true.

Leaving Blackburn had been a terrible wrench. I asked Jo how long it took her to return, and what she felt when finally she did. She began by telling me where her new life had led her.

'We ended up moving from lodgings to lodgings, which made me feel very insecure. I had to change school every six months and, to make it worse, Mum took up with this chap... She used to cry a lot, and although I hated the fact that she stayed with him, I knew she did so to give us some stability.'

Among the places they stayed was an estate in Ridgmont. Readers will recall pretty, strong-willed Nell Reece making a similar flight in *Cradle of Thorns*, which is appropriate since henceforth Jo would have to have Nell's self-sufficiency and strength, together with all the Christian values that are rewarded in the novel:

> The journey to Ridgmont was painstakingly slow. There were few signs along the narrow, meandering lanes, and Nell had to stop and ask the way several times.
>
> At last, just as the sun was beginning to lose its glory, she came into Ridgmont hamlet by way of the Ampthill Road. 'My! This is a lovely place,' she remarked, looking from one side of the street to the other. The old square church with its pretty tower stood to the left of her, and to the right was an ancient inn with black-timbered gables and flower-filled gardens. Both sides of the street were lined with quaint cottages. Children played outside. There were bairns in prams and mothers chatting, and a lazy, easy feeling to the place that immediately put Nell at ease.

Here, Jo made friends with a girl called Marion, and then one day she met someone who was to change her life completely – 'This tall, blond man came striding cross the road,' Jo recalls. 'He turned out to be Ken, Marion's brother! They say there's no such thing as love at first sight, but I knew Ken was the man for me as soon as I laid eyes on him. Unfortunately he didn't feel the same. He thought I was too young for him. I wasn't yet 16. I used to hang around waiting for him all the time, but he would say, "Go away, you're just a snotty-nosed kid." I would be following him everywhere and I was so young. I was smitten, he was so smart, I just fell in love with him as soon as I saw him. Then we just became friends. I was friends with his sister and we'd just start chatting, you know?

'Then we went to my Auntie Biddy's in Dunstable. My Uncle Fred, that's Auntie Biddy's husband, worked in the rubber factory there, and Auntie Biddy, who was a very stern lady, very disciplined, quite frightening to me and yet she had a heart of gold, she insisted that as I had left school at 14 – you could if you had to earn a living – I should go and work in the rubber factory. But Uncle Fred thought it was absolutely not on the cards for me to work

'How much she longed to walk again the streets and ginnels of her beloved Blackburn.'
Let Loose The Tigers

Converted street community, 1960s. When Jo returned to Blackburn, she was appalled by the clearance programme. 'In the 1960s, they razed it to the ground and built these square, horrible blocks!' The town's two-decade clearance plan brought a cry for a stay of execution from townspeople who didn't want their terraced-house communities destroyed. The programme was halted and the overall strategy modified to include grants for renovation of existing dwellings.

at the rubber factory – not the place for a young girl – and there was quite an argument. But Auntie Biddy was adamant, I was to go and work in that rubber factory. Mum had gone into hospital to have the baby and I ran away and found my way to Ken. I had already met his family, so I ran away to his Mum. I walked all the way from Dunstable back to Ridgmont!'

Two years after leaving Blackburn she returned with Ken, 'to meet me dad and me brothers and that. Me dad was a little bit hostile towards him, he wasn't warm like he normally was. Maybe because I was only 16 and he knew that Ken was the one...a father's protective instincts. Then, later, when I wrote to him and told him that Ken and I were getting married, and I would be so proud for him to come and give me away, he wrote, "I am not giving you away. You are too young. I will not be there." My father refused to come to my wedding. He thought I was too young to get married. He refused to come and give me away. That really did upset me. He should have been by my side. Instead of that, it was a relative of Ken's. My father wouldn't even give his permission, my mother did, my mam gave her blessing...but that broke my heart, the fact that he wouldn't come

'The flagstones on the pavement were grey and crooked just like they had always been, and the gas-lamps where they had lassoed their ropes and swung round and round stood strong and straight, just as when he was a boy. Time had marched on but these things remained the same. Nothing else in the street had changed. Only him. And Phoebe. And his need for her.'
Jessica's Girl

down and give me away. We were married on Easter Saturday 1958. I was 16 and Ken was 19.'

Today, with two adult sons, Spencer and Wayne, Jo and Ken are as close as ever – 'He's my best friend and right arm,' she says. 'It could all have gone so wrong, but we grew up together.'

Almost three decades of growing up, and more hardship and loss, were to pass before first publication of *Her Father's Sins*. 'In those years a succession of things happened to us,' Jo recalls. 'We both lost our parents, then I lost a young brother. For two years our bad luck just went on and on... I came out the other end realising you have to be grateful for what you have – and that if you want anything, you must go out and get it.'

In the 1970s Ken's haulage business – possibly the genesis of Harry Jenkins' company in *Living a Lie* – secured against their house, succumbed to the recession and Jo and he lost their home. They went to live with Ken's parents, one son moving in with other relatives owing to lack of space. 'We lost everything. We had nothing again,' says Jo. 'But we picked ourselves up, dusted ourselves down, and got on with it. You either go down and stay down, or you get up and fight back. It was a really rough time.

'We had to beg the council to give us a house. All they could offer was an unbelievably filthy, semi-derelict house. There was graffiti on the walls, people had broken in, windows were missing, the roof had caved in and anything of value had been ripped out. We ran from this place, but the Authorities said if we didn't take this we wouldn't get any house. So we rolled up our sleeves and renovated it from top to bottom. The neighbours were using the garden as a tip – we must have taken out about six skip-loads of rubbish when we first moved in. It took a long time to get the place right, but in the end we grew to love it. We lived there for seventeen years.'

When the boys started school, Jo took O and A levels while at the same time making belts for plastic macs – 'I went for three years to evening classes after working in a plastics factory all day. It felt wonderful; I'd ask for extra assignments. I did very well and got A-levels in Sociology, English and History, with A grades and distinctions, though I found the O level maths lessons very hard because I had in mind that frightening maths teacher at school in Blackburn! I'd already applied for teacher-training at Bletchley College, got my teaching Cert. and then I was offered a place at Lucy Cavendish College, Cambridge.'

Lucy Cavendish is the only college of Cambridge University to offer (exclusively) mature women returnees the opportunity to pursue a higher education that they may have deferred or interrupted. Acceptance was a quite extraordinary achievement – from dodging lessons in Blackburn's Corporation Park, and feeling the sting of her father's leather belt when she got home, to being offered a place as an undergraduate at the most prestigious university in

Britain. However, in true, pragmatic style, Jo turned the offer down. Going to Cambridge would have meant living on site and splitting up the family. There was nothing more likely to concentrate Jo's mind than home. Instead she began teaching to O and A levels in English and History at a local Comprehensive school.

Meanwhile, visits to Blackburn had continued. She was appalled by the town clearance programme. 'When I was growing up in Blackburn the centre had these lovely old buildings,' she said to me. 'Then, in the 1960s, they razed it to the ground and built these square, horrible blocks! The re-building was all going on when I was away, and I was shocked when I went back, and Derwent Street had gone, a complete area, a whole minefield of streets! They had all the flats there off Montague Street, and the first thing I thought was, where's the bike shop, the little old man who used to hire bikes out of there at fourpence a day? Where had he gone? As a kid I would work all weekend collecting newspapers to take to the factory to get my fourpence and then I would go to the shop and hire my bike,

'I was shocked when I went back, and Derwent Street had gone, a complete area, a whole minefield of streets....and the first thing I thought was, where's the bike shop, the little old man who used to hire bikes out of there at 4d a day? Where had he gone?'

Collecting her feelings, she paused. 'I began thinking about Blackburn and everything, and it was as though I'd left something behind.' She gave a small bitter laugh. 'It's hard to explain, but it was my life.' Angry tears filled her eyes. 'And they took it away.'

Somewhere, Someday

'Folks seemed to have more brass in their pockets too, in spite of the fact that many of the old familiar cotton mills had been closed down.'

Let Loose The Tigers

proudly take it home to cycle to Accrington to see my grandad. I remember once I came out and my sister had pinched my bike and gone off on it and brought it back two minutes before it had to be returned. I hated her! Winifred, older than me by about two and a half years. She was quite a horror! Yet now, she's my best friend. The worst thing they did to Blackburn was to take the market. They took the whole market area away, the clock and everything.'

I asked whether Mary Jane, her mother, had ever returned to the town.

'Yes she did, but not until after my dad died. I don't recall her going up there for a long long time. Oh, how I remember her at Cicely Bridge Mill. Do you know, I watched it being knocked down. Ken and I went up there. I showed him where me mam worked and where I pushed the little babbies in the pram to meet her when I was about nine. We got about half way up and there was this cordon across the road and all these cranes and things. I got out and had a look and it was half demolished. I couldn't believe they were taking

'The worst thing they did to Blackburn was to take the market. They took the whole market area away, the clock and everything.'

it down... I stood and cried. Did you read *Let Loose the Tigers*, when they were pulling this street down and Queenie cried, not because they were knocking a street down but because they were knocking her history down? Where flesh and blood had lived and breathed and slept and worked, and it was going and it would be no more. That – the way she felt – is exactly how I felt that day when I saw them knock down Cicely Bridge Mill.

'The whole time I was teaching, I had wanted to write,' recalls Jo. 'It was always at the back of my mind.' Then at some point in 1984, just a year after Cicely Bridge Cotton Mill was closed, Jo was in bed recovering from an operation when a visiting teaching colleague said, 'Why don't you write that book you're always on about?' Given the opportunity Jo seized it at last.

'I wrote stories about the people I grew up with. Once I started, the words just flowed off the pages. I'd be writing when the nurse came to switch off the light, then I'd switch it back on again and carry on writing. I wrote the first book in six weeks – *Her Father's Sins*. It was a bestseller in 1987, it really was an overnight bestseller,' she recalls, with as much delight as when first she was informed.

'The same year the publishers accepted it, Ken and the two boys entered me into a *Mirror* Group 'Superwoman of Britain' competition right across the nation to find someone who had come through to do well against all obstacles. I think there were 4,000 contestants. I knew nothing about it until one day I picked up the phone and someone said, "Josephine Cox, please. I'd like to interview her."

'I said, "What for? Who are you?" And she said she had to interview me. I had eight interviews. They had 4,000 entries and they whittled it down to twelve and the twelve went off to the Dorchester Hotel. Then Derek Nimmo and a whole panel of people interviewed us one after another. Three or four days – absolutely out of this world! Then we were all told to line up in the Savoy Hotel. Third, second... and then they called out my name. I couldn't believe it! I won £1,000 and a silver rose bowl. What a way to launch the book!'

Jo had not answered my question, what it had felt like going back to Blackburn for the first time, except to say that she had returned many times. I know that today she goes back regularly to see family, and likes nothing better than to laugh with friends about the old times.

For the writer there is a serious inability to bury the past and such a desire to re-visit it that the past often seems more real than the present. The answer to my question may be that Jo only truly returned to Blackburn when she visited it imaginatively in *Her Father's Sins*, and I put it to her that of all the novels that involve

the heroine making a return to Blackburn, *Somewhere, Someday* seems the most true in terms of emotional response.

Kelly Wilson suffers a similar loss to Jo, though an even more dramatic one. Her father, the source of strife, has been murdered in the family house (No. 12 Johnson Street in the novel, which is Addison Street in reality). Her mother goes to prison for the murder, Kelly leaves Blackburn.

I spent time at the top of Addison Street, which meets Preston New Road on the north boundary of the mill-colony in which Jo was born. It is one of those high-up places from which Jo's heroines look out over Blackburn and drink deep of the spirit of the place.

'This street you are talking about in *Somewhere, Someday*,' Jo said to me. 'I used to play in that street when I was a child, and it is on a real steep brew, you know? Stand at the top and you can see right across the whole of Blackburn. I called it Johnson Street, but it is Addison Street in real life. The family of the children I played with used to live in the house at the very top. We were on a tour up north about four years ago and as we drove past the top of the street I saw this house all boarded up. And I thought where have they gone? And if they've moved on, why is that house not being lived in? And it played on my mind because it was part of my life. So that is where the story came from. I thought, I am going to have someone going back to that house.'

Kelly returns to Blackburn, the site of her childhood trauma. 'I poured my own emotions into her going back,' Jo admits. 'You know, when I came back to see my father for the first time after he and my mam separated, there really was a milkman coming round the corner...'

She watched the milkman as he swung into the street, then reined in his horse to serve the many customers who stood, jug in hand, each awaiting her turn. He chatted awhile, and laughingly chucked the bairns under the chin, before measuring out the milk from his churn with a ladle... In her memory's eye, Kelly could see herself in that queue. A small girl carrying a jug almost as big as herself, she would dare to touch the horse's chest and pat his face when he looked down. If he kissed her for an apple, she would screech with delight. Such vivid, precious times.

Like Jo, when Kelly returns there are ghosts to lay, 'and the feelings were the same, they were transported into that street, what Kelly felt was what I felt.'

Kelly returns to Blackburn, the site of childhood trauma, as did Jo: 'I poured my own emotions into her going back,' Jo admits. 'You know, when I came back to see my father for the first time after he and my mam separated...'

'When the moment came, and she was standing at the top of Johnson [Addison] Street, Kelly was filled with a strange kind of calm, as though it wasn't her standing there, but someone else. Someone she didn't even know.'
Somewhere, Someday

When the moment came, and she was standing at the top of Johnson Street, Kelly was filled with a strange kind of calm, as though it wasn't her standing there, but someone else. Someone she didn't even know.

Mesmerised, she gazed at each house in turn; all but one.

Deliberately she turned her back to it – the house where she and her brother had lived with their parents; the house she had loved, the house she had feared. If she were to stretch out her arm now, she could touch it, and she would. She must! But, fearing her own emotions, she prolonged the inevitable.

Like an old friend, or enemy, it called to her, daring her to turn and see. She so wanted to look at the house, at the small, significant things. She hoped the words her brother had scratched into the windowsill had lasted the test of time. Michael and Kelly for ever – he had written it with their mother's kitchen knife. No one had noticed; no one knew except she and her brother. Was it still there? Dare she look?

She remembered the door too, solid and permanent, as if it might be left standing long after the house and everyone in it had fallen away. She needed to see if the door was the same one that her father had put on after the old one warped with the weather; the door with the big, dark keyhole and a letter-box that sang in the wind. The door through which she and her loved ones had passed time and again.

It was stark in her mind now, that wonderfully familiar door made of dark, solid wood, with four panels and a small brass knocker in the shape of a crown. Oh yes, she longed to look on it, but try as she might, she did not quite dare.

Instead she roved her eyes over other familiar things: grubby, stone-framed windows; paving flags in long straight lines like little soldiers, some more worn than others; lampposts with stiff, inviting arms; and a road filled with plump misshapen cobblestones that resembled new-baked loaves. Little had changed.

Choking back a well of emotion, Kelly devoured it all. She had forgotten how it felt. Until now, she had not realised how much it meant to her.

After a moment, she raised her gaze and looked beyond the street to the distant view. As she did so, her heart turned somersaults.

Kelly had always thought this to be the most wonderful view in the world. Even though she had been a long time away, it had stayed in her mind's eye, etched on her soul for ever.

Now, in this unforgettable moment, she drank it in, her soul crying out with excitement. Almost as though she was being lifted from the ground, she felt herself fly, soaring with the view, down and away, over the heart of Blackburn town and beyond, to the hills. She saw the church spires and the towering cotton-mills, the endless, shifting sky spreading its fluttering wings over all below, and her quiet eyes knew it all.

This was what she remembered... grimy, smoky Blackburn town; so beautiful, it took her breath away.

'How I've missed you,' she sighed, and her heart was broken.

BOOKS by JOSEPHINE COX

1987 Her Father's Sins
1988 Let Loose The Tigers
1989 Angels Cry Sometimes
1989 Take This Woman
1990 Whistledown Woman
1991 Outcast
1991 Alley Urchin
1992 Vagabonds
1992 Don't Cry Alone
1993 Jessica's Girl
1993 Nobody's Darling
1994 Born To Serve
1994 More Than Riches
1995 A Little Badness
1995 Living a Lie
1996 The Devil You Know
1996 A Time For Us
1997 Cradle of Thorns
1997 Miss You Forever
1998 Love Me Or Leave Me
1998 Tomorrow The World
1999 The Gilded Cage
1999 Somewhere, Someday
2000 Rainbow Days
2000 Looking Back
2001 Let it Shine
2001 The Woman Who Left

As Jane Brindle
1991 Scarlet
1992 No Mercy
1994 The Tallow Image
1995 No Heaven, No Hell
1997 The Seeker
1998 The Hiding Game

INDEX

Accrington 63
Accrington Road 40
Addison Street 8, 187, 188
Ainsworth Street 42, 92
Albert Mill 24
Alma Mill 28
Alley Urchin 23, 24, 54, 56, 65, 124
Angela's Ashes 174
Angels Cry Sometimes 26, 29, 32, 34, 35, 39, 40, 42, 51, 77, 80, 91, 95, 97, 98, 102, 106, 131, 133, 141, 146, 162, 165, 170, 172, 176
Arkwright, Richard 121, 122
Aspects of Blackburn 124, 141
Aspen, Chris 128

Baldwin, William 151
Baron, John 105
Barrel organ grinder 42
Bay Horse Hotel 127
Beattie, Derek 97, 123, 127, 145, 150, 153, 154, 159
Belasyse, Thomas Viscount Falconbergh 151
Bennington Street 92
Bent Street 69
Beveridge Report 165
Billington, William 147, 148, 149, 155, 161
Birley Street 62
Blackburn: The Development of a Lancashire Cotton Town 97
Blackburn Rovers FC 16, 26, 94
Blackburn Standard 142, 144, 158, 167
Blackpool 70-77
Blakewater River, 15, 49, 142
Blakey Moor 103
Bletchley College 181
Born To Serve 156
Boulevard, The 51, 52, 53, 54, 79
Brierley, Ellen 111
Brindle, Jane, *see also* Family, 178
Brookhouse Mill 18, 44, 78, 80
Brown Street/Bridge 52, 54
Bullen, Sheila 46
Bullough, James 122
Buncer Lane 62

Cambridge University 181, 182
Canal, Leeds-Liverpool 28, 32, 116, 117, 123-126
Cardwell Mill 24
Cartwright, Revd Edmund 122
Castle, Barbara 154
Cathedral, Blackburn 15
Charlton, John 108
Chartism 158-160
Cherry Tree 68, 83, 160
Child labour 132-138
China 127, 162
Christmas 70
Church Street 16, 50, 131, 132
Cicely Bridge Mill 11, 26, 28, 30, 32, 54, 90, 116, 137, 183, 185
Cicely Bridge 29, 31, 32
Cicely Hill 30
Cicely Lane 123
Civil War, American 84, 141-4
English 16
Clayton Manor 161, 162
Cleaver Street 144
Clemesha, Robert 108, 155
Clitheroe 15
Coal industry 132, 163
Colne 109
Corn Laws 127
Corporation, The (pub) 85
Corporation Park 7, 26, 81-87
Cotton Industry, The 128
Cotton process 119-122
Cox, *see* Family
Cradle of Thorns 24, 46, 54, 61, 64, 65, 80, 138, 139, 148, 178
Crompton, Samuel 122

Dandy Mill 123
Darwen Street/Bridge 15, 167
Derwent Street 20, 21, 22, 26, 28, 38, 49, 69, 103, 166, 182
Device, Alison 109
Devil You Know, The 58
Dickens, Charles 69, 92
Dickinson, William 122
Dorchester Hotel, London 185
Don't Cry Alone 52, 56, 62, 63, 79, 91, 119, 132, 139, 174, 176
Drunkenness 79-81, 90, 102, 155, 166-172, 174-178
Dugdale, Richard 105
Dutton's brewery 115, 141, 165
Duke of York pub 167
Dunstable 173, 178, 179

Eanam Wharf 117, 118
Education, *see also* Child labour, Mechanics' Institution, Sunday School, Technical College, School, Truancy, 69-70, 139
Education Acts 138, 139

Factory Acts 136, 138
Fair, Blackburn 16, 97-102
Family, Josephine Cox's family
Barney (father) 26, 64, 179
Bernard (brother) 23, 49, 85, 92
Betty (aunt) 40
Biddy (aunt) 24, 70, 178
Fred (uncle) 178
Ken (husband) 11, 178, 179, 181, 183
Margaret (aunt) 23
Marion (sister-in-law) 178
Mary Jane (mother) 24, 25, 26, 29, 32, 59, 102, 173-174
Richard (brother) 23
Spencer (son) 181
Wayne (son) 181
Winifred (sister) 77, 100, 183
Faucher, Leon 128
Feilden family 150
Henry 151
Joseph 84
Feilden's Arms, Mellor Brook 150
Feilden Street 59
Finn, Rosie 26
Flying shuttle 120
Forest of Bowland 89
Forest of Pendle 109, 111
Francis, Graham 16
Further Gate 158, 159

Gandhi, Mahatma 164
Gaspey, William 158
Graham, Hugh Gardiner 146
Grammar School, Queen Elizabeth's 137, 152
Griffin pub 26
Grimshaw Park 18
Gypsy 56, 74

Halloween 114
Hargreaves, James 121, 122, 127
Hartley, John 127
Haslingden Road 138
Hattersley & Sons 122
Health 19, 131
Henry Street 26, 51, 52, 53, 54, 59, 63, 64, 106, 177
Henry Street, Church 26
Her Father's Sins, 9, 19, 20, 22, 24, 38, 43, 45, 46, 56, 66, 68, 70, 74, 80, 93, 131, 145, 155, 166, 181, 185
Heyes, Jim 141
Hodgson, Joseph 105
Hoghton, Sir Gilbert 16
Hoghton Tower 16
Hornby, Harry 153
Horrocks, William 122
Housing 18, 20, 21, 166
Hull, George 105, 106, 149

India 127, 162, 164
Infirmary, Blackburn 131, 133

Jackson, Colonel Robert Raynsford 161, 162
Japan 162
Jazz Band Night 90
Jessica's Girl 22, 36, 44, 47, 53, 78, 112, 141, 156, 181
Johnston Street 63

Kay, John 120
Kenworthy, William 122
King Edward VII 152
King George VI 11
King Street 15, 17, 26, 28, 49, 64, 65, 78, 97
King Street Mill 122
King William Street 57, 108
King's Head pub 167
Knocker-up 28, 31

Lancaster Castle 111
Lancet, The 164
Larkhill 62, 63, 166
Let Loose The Tigers 44, 72, 75, 76, 165, 179, 183, 185
Library, Blackburn 131, 192
Little Badness, A 61, 138
Liverpool 53, 119
Living a Lie 169, 176, 181
Longfellow, Henry Wadsworth 104
Looking Back 26, 65, 80, 98, 101, 124, 131, 155, 175
Love Me Or Leave Me 81, 82, 85, 90
Lucy Cavendish College 181
Lytham St Anne's 44

Magistrate's Court 167
Manchester 15, 165
Market 10, 53-58, 108, 140
McCourt, Frank 174
Mating, Marriage & the Status of Women 168
Mechanics' Institution 147
Mellor 126, 150
Mill Hill 23, 24
Miss You Forever 138
Montague Street 29, 46, 167
More Than Riches 85
Mosley, Oswald 155
Muffin-man 114
Museum & Art Gallery, Blackburn 131, 192

National Health Service 165
National Insurance Act 162
Navigation (pub) 24, 25, 64
Nazareth House 11, 66, 67-68
Nimmo, Derek 185
Nobody's Darling 26, 60, 78, 80, 82, 85, 178
Normans 15
Northgate 15
Nova Scotia Mill 18

Oakenhurst Road 26
Oestler, Richard 166
Outcast 24, 82, 86, 112, 114, 115, 116, 117, 118, 125, 142

Paradise Lane 152
Parkinson Street 22, 23, 24

Paul, Lewis 122
Pawn shop 162
Peel, Sir Robert 127
Peel's Mill 127
Pendle Hill 111, 114
Pendle witches 111-114
Penny Street 51
Perrault, Charles 112
Peter Street 95
Pigeons 94
Pilgrim Trust, The 77
Pilkington family 131
Platt Brothers 122
Pleasington 83, 154
Poets, Blackburn 104-109, 146-149
Poets & Poetry of Blackburn 105
Police 90, 91, 159, 167
Poor Laws 157
Population 123
Poverty 17, 22, 60-62, 66-71, 80, 127, 131, 144-149, 157-158, 162-166, 172
Preston New Road 26, 43, 66, 68, 83, 87, 114, 115, 131, 162, 185
Prince, J C 108
Prince's Street 26, 59
Princess Street 17
Property agents 62
Pump Street 66

Queen Alexandra 152
Queen's Park Hospital 138, 139

Rag-and-bone merchant 42, 43, 59, 60, 62
Ragged School 10, 11, 67, 68, 69-71
Railway 123-4
Railway Road 117
Railway Station 32, 52, 53, 54
Rainbow Days 26
Rawcliffe, Richard 106, 107
Reform Bill 155
Regent Street 51, 54, 59
Religion, *see also* Nazareth House, Ragged School, Sunday School 26, 59, 67, 112, 138
Rialto cinema 96, 97
Ribble Valley/River 15, 16, 105
Ribchester 15, 16, 104, 105, 106
Ridgmont 178, 179
Road To Nab End, The 78, 112, 162
Romans 15

St Anne's school 26, 59, 60
Salford/Bridge 15, 17, 53, 131, 142
Salvation Army 71
Samlesbury/Hall 87, 111, 112, 147
Samlesbury witches 112
Sanitation 19, 21, 131
Savoy Hotel, London 185
Saxons 15
Scarlet 178
School 26, 59, 92-94, 136-138, 178, 181
Shear Brow 15
Ship, The (pub) 52
Slipper Baths 94-97
Soho Foundry 123
Somewhere, Someday 8, 50, 62, 85, 168, 182, 187, 188
Soup kitchen 144
Southern, Elizabeth 109
Southworth, Jane 111
  Sir John 112
  Christopher 112
Sowerbutts, Grace 112
Spinning, *see* Cotton process
Spinning jenny 121
Spinning mule 122
Stancliffe Street 18
Stanhill 121
Stapley Bridge 158
Stephen Street 23
Straw, Jack 155
Sudell family
  Henry 150
  William 151
Sun, The (pub) 26, 64, 65
Sunday School 70, 147
Swan, The (pub) 64, 65
Swimming baths 95

Take This Woman 21, 26, 56, 176
Technical College 152, 162
Teddy's Shop 97
Three Pigeons (pub) 26
Thwaites brewery 115, 141, 142, 165
Thwaites, Daniel 153
Time For Us, A 112, 127
Tiplady, Charles 50, 54, 131, 132, 155, 158, 159
Tolpuddle Martyrdom 157
Tomorrow The World 28, 29, 54, 64, 78, 127, 156, 170, 171
Truancy 40, 90

Union Street Bridge 54

Vagabonds 24, 125, 147
Violence 17, 50, 80-81, 111, 158, 167-172, 176-178

War, First World 162, 163
  Second World 20, 92, 165
Water frame 121
Waterfall Mill 24, 66
Weaving, *see* Cotton process
Wensley Fold Mill 18, 122
Whalley Banks/Mill 49, 122
Whistledown Valley 87
Whistledown Woman 54, 87, 112
Whitekirk 92
Whittaker, Revd John 166
Whittle, Anne 109
Wilpshire 83, 162
Winstanley, Michael 133, 135
Witchcraft 109-114
Witton 83
Witton House 151
Witton Mill 18
Woman Who Left, The 24, 87, 174
Working Children in 19th-Century Lancashire 133
Woodfold Hall 150
Woodruff, William 78, 112, 127, 155, 162, 164
Workhouse 138, 139

Yates, Henry 104, 146, 149

ACKNOWLEDGEMENTS

I would like to thank Diana Rushton and Alan Duckworth at the Local Studies Department of the Blackburn Library, who supplied many of the black and white photographs and maps. Besides Charles Tiplady's recently recovered, 19th-century *Diary* of the town, Alan Duckworth's *Aspects of Blackburn* was essential research. Similar help and source material came from Nick Harling at the Blackburn Museum & Art Gallery and from Albert Branscombe of the Local History Society.

I have already acknowledged Derek Beattie's *Blackburn: The Development of a Lancashire Cotton Town* (Ryburn Publishing, 1992) as the most authoritative modern history, and repeat my indebtedness to his research and acumen. *Poets and Poetry of Blackburn, 1793-1902* by George Hull (J & G Toulmin, 1902) was another eye-opener; working-class Blackburn poets draw together so many of the themes of the present book. Other crucial sources were *The Road To Nab End* by William Woodruff (Eland, 1993), *Working Children in 19th-Century Lancashire*, edited by Michael Winstanley (Lancashire County Books, 1995), *20th-Century Blackburn* by Andrew Taylor (Wharncliffe Books, 2000), and *Images of East Lancashire* by Eric Leaver (copyright *Lancashire Evening Telegraph*, published by Breedon Books, 1993).

The colour map is by Martin Collins, colour photography by myself. Among the black and whites the stunning street scenes of the 1960s by Shirley Baker deserve special mention. Readers may know her books, *Street Photographs. Manchester & Salford* (Bloodaxe, 1989) and *Streets & Spaces* (Lowry Press, 2000). Other photographic sources to whom I am indebted include the British Waterways Board; the Documentary Photographic Archive of the Greater Manchester County Record Office; the *Guardian* Media Group plc; Lancashire County Library: Burnley Library; *The Lancashire Evening Telegraph*; the Manchester Local Studies Unit, Central Library, Manchester; the North West Film Archive, Manchester; and Oldham Metropolitan Borough Leisure Services, Local Studies Library.

Above all, I would like to thank Josephine Cox, whose contribution lies at the very heart of the book.